Governor Hu

May God Bless your

journey to the White House.

You truly are a

Mindsetter.

Blessings,

Pamela Roberts

BE A
MINDSETTER

THE ESSENTIAL GUIDE TO **INSPIRE, INFLUENCE** AND **IMPACT** OTHERS

Published by
LID Publishing Ltd
Garden Studios, 71-75 Shelton Street
Covent Garden, London WC2H 9JQ

31 West 34th Street, Suite 7004,
New York, NY 10001, US

info@lidpublishing.com
www.lidpublishing.com

www.BeAMindsetter.com

A member of:

BPR
Business Publishers Roundtable
www.businesspublishersroundtable.com

Printed in Great Britain by CPI Group (UK) Ltd.
ISBN: 978-1-910649-20-6

Cover and page design: Laura Hawkins

BE A
MINDSETTER

THE ESSENTIAL GUIDE
TO **INSPIRE, INFLUENCE**
AND **IMPACT** OTHERS

MICHAEL GOBRAN | WILLIAM GREENWALD | DEREK ROBERTS

LONDON   MONTERREY
MADRID   SHANGHAI
MEXICO CITY   BOGOTA
NEW YORK   BUENOS AIRES
BARCELONA   SAN FRANCISCO

TO OUR SPOUSES AND CHILDREN:
We are so appreciative of the time we borrowed from each of you during our writing journey. We owe an incalculable debt to you, and we remain forever grateful for the unconditional belief, grace, support and confidence you have freely given to us. Our work would not exist without you by our sides all along the way.

CONTENTS

FOREWORD

As the creator of the FISH! Philosophy, I had the privilege to co-author the international bestselling book *FISH!*. It has inspired millions of people around the world. In the book, I talk about four practices to boost morale and improve results. One of them is "Choose your attitude." For me, this is the core practice and the starting point for everything in life and at work.

I truly believe that having the right attitude multiplies the success of any individual, team, organization or community. That's why it's so important to do everything possible to establish or strengthen a desirable mindset.

You see, the way we think – our mindset – changes the way we live, work, relate to others within our community, and value life itself. Not only that, but I believe each person has the power to influence and change his or her own personal mindset. And when mindsets shift, people can purposefully shift themselves toward new outcomes and new ways of living.

Unfortunately, choosing our attitudes or changing our mindsets is not easy. Each of us needs all the support we can get – support from our community, support from within ourselves, support from tools or just from friends.

This is why I am so excited about the book you're holding.

We all know that *how* we communicate plays a big role in the success we have in sharing our thoughts. As human beings, we aren't simply input/output machines. We are complex creatures. However, at the core of every complex task lies a simple format. The 3R-Axiom© that is introduced in this book is exactly that. It is a simple, yet powerful, methodology that will forever change how you communicate and share your ideas.

I want to encourage you to take this book to heart, to embrace the 3R-Methodology, to build your own powerful message using its interactive format, and to become a Mindsetter for your friends, your family, your community and even the world.

I believe we all have the power to inspire others and shape the world around us. We have done this for millions of people through our FISH! Philosophy. The good news is that you can do this too with your own philosophy – your own personal mindset. The way you see and think and act can inspire those around you in ways you may never know if you don't step out in action and begin sharing your mindset.

It's worth the effort. Because in the end, mindset is what really matters.

JOHN CHRISTENSEN,
CREATOR OF THE FISH! PHILOSOPHY
AND CEO OF CHARTHOUSE LEARNING, INC

INTRODUCTION

IT'S ALL ABOUT MAKING AN IMPACT
AND NOT JUST AN IMPRESSION

"The two words 'information' and 'communication' are often used interchangeably," says journalist Sydney Harris, "but they signify quite different things. **Information is giving out; communication is getting through.**'"

Every day, you and those around you are bombarded with information. Technology such as smartphones, cable television, mobile tablets and the pervasive nature of the internet mean we're more connected than ever. For example, a recent study[1] by the Radicati Group reports that the average office worker sends and receives more than 100 emails daily, while Pew Research[2] estimates that the typical cell phone user sends an average of 1,500 text messages every month. As technology continues to rapidly advance our ability to stay connected 24/7, these numbers will likely be higher by the time you read this.

Does all of this information mean we're **communicating** more, or are we being drowned in a steady stream of information that creates no real impact, no real behavioural change and simply goes in one ear and out the other?

Teachers trying to help students learn and experience facts, and not just memorize them, recognize today's problem. Trainers and motivational speakers who are passionate about helping people improve their lives know the struggle. "But I'm not a speaker or teaching professional like that," you may say to yourself. And yet, you are – every single day.

At the workplace, you may find yourself trying to build skills and values into your team. At home, you want your children to make good decisions and you want to arm them with the emotional tools necessary to navigate our complex world. Throughout the day, we are all constantly trying to impart a specific message to those around us.

Unfortunately, despite our best efforts, we're often only a pusher of content and mover of information. We fail to actually affect change and make an impact on those in our workplace, family and community.

Thankfully, fixing this is simple. You don't need to go to a public speaking class. You don't need a college degree for extra letters after your name. In fact, there's a guaranteed way to make your words and messages truly have an impact. **And you can start doing it today, with the book you're holding.**

Three cutting-edge experts have combined their knowledge and experience to present you with a simple, proven and extremely effective method to communicate your ideas and thoughts in a way that will change minds and lives – no matter your message.

Derek Roberts is an executive communication consultant, speaker and leadership coach with expertise in organizational change management and the development of high-performing sales and business development teams. **William Greenwald** is founder and

Chief NeuroLeaderologist[3] of a global executive development and leadership coaching firm specializing in the neuropsychology of team and leadership behaviour. **Michael Gobran** is an executive coach and leadership trainer as well as the co-founder of a Web 2.0 platform that helps anyone create and communicate impactful information instantly and automatically.

While these individuals come from different fields, a common vision and mission drew them together for this book:

- To see people's mindsets significantly and sustainably impacted for the better

- To empower others to share the messages that are within them in a way that meaningfully inspires, influences and impacts others

- To share with the world a simple methodology that can be replicated by anyone who wants to craft effective communication

These three experts are united in a belief that mindset matters. Each of our mindsets play a big role in our success, personally and professionally. Adopting a positive mindset is a choice and a learned skill, and Mindsetters like you make the difference.

What you're holding in your hands is the key to taking **information** and turning it into **communication.** It's written as a short fictional story, with your message as the story's main character.

The authors have named him "SAM," and there's a very specific reason for his name that you'll learn in Section 1.

Along the way, your message will meet other messages competing for the recipient's attention. SAM, and you by extension, will discover what it takes to achieve true communication — all while he tries to avoid something ominous called The Forgetting.

Personal experiences from the authors, as well as insights into ground- breaking research on learning and forgetting, are woven throughout the book. The intent is to demonstrate what it takes to change behaviour and show how you can help someone internalize what you have said. By the time you're done, you'll uncover three simple-yet-radical axioms (Reduce, Relate, Reflect). When combined into one methodology we call it the 3R-Axiom and you can apply it to almost anything you are trying to say.

As you journey through the book, the authors will walk you through basic exercises and worksheets to help you hone and perfect your message. This is not a workbook, but a working book.

When you reach the story's end, you'll be able to inspire and change minds, influence behaviours and truly communicate what's in your heart and on your mind in a way that's effective and proven by the latest research and field experience.

It's easier than you think, and you'll see the benefits in every area of your life no matter your occupation, interests or hobbies. This is your chance to cut through the information clutter and revolutionize your communication today. This is your chance to become a Mindsetter!

SECTION 1

REDUCE

THE **FIRST** "R" OF THE 3R-AXIOM

Make SAM...

CHAPTER 1

Dylan Jackson saw his friend's shoulders slumped, heavy with the invisible weight of his recent divorce. Dylan knew he needed to find a way to speak joy and hope into his friend's life before it was too late.

Tim Martinez felt a tinge of nervousness as he grabbed the doorknob. Behind this door was the board of directors for a local company. If he did well during the meeting, the children's hospital would receive a much-needed grant from the local company. If he couldn't get them to see his vision and passion, the hospital would be forced to cut crucial services.

Catherine Mitchell watched her daughter texting away rapidly on her smartphone. She knew parenting a teenager would be rough, but she never imagined it would be this tough. Her daughter was struggling with some big life issues, and Catherine knew that if she couldn't find a better way to communicate, her daughter could go down a dangerous life path.

These three real people — whose names have been changed to protect their privacy — knew that everything hinged upon the success of their message getting through to the people that mattered the most to them.

You know how it feels, too — when every word counts, and you only have one shot at getting it right. You've been in these situations where you have a chance to be a Mindsetter, helping to shape someone's mindset and dramatically influencing the course of a person's life, a child's dreams or an organization's trajectory.

Maybe you're in that kind of situation right now.

This book is a guide and an interactive tool for you to develop and test your own messages. Throughout the chapters, we will challenge you to write down your thoughts and refine them in the context of our 3R-Axiom so that by the end of the book your message will be well-crafted and equipped for survival. If you are ready for this journey, then let's get started.

First, can you think of a time when it seemed like everything depended on you and your ability to deliver just the right message? What words did you choose? How did you craft your message?

Now, take a moment to think about your current situation. Do you have something that you want or need to share? What is your core message? How are you going to make sure that it gets through to your audience?

As you reflect on these questions, please write your thoughts below:

MY SITUATION THAT I'D LIKE TO SPEAK INTO:

_____

_____

THE PERSON/PEOPLE THAT I'M TRYING TO HELP:

_____

_____

THE MESSAGE THAT I WANT TO SHARE WITH THOSE I CARE ABOUT:

_____

_____

Now, think about what happens to this message once you release it. How will it be heard and received? More importantly, will your message survive and take root in the recipient's mind where it can transform, grow and produce optimal results?

The story you'll read next is about your message itself — your life-changing, dreams-shifting, passion-building message.

This is a tale of what happens when your message finds itself in a recipient's mind, fighting against all odds to survive and avoid being forgotten and get where it needs to go.

It's a story about bringing your message to life, and your message's survival and success depends on you. Will your message survive, going on to build up and strengthen a desired mindset?

You can't run when you're tired...

...Though his eyes burned and his body ached, SAM's mind kept returning to that thought. *The tired ones always get taken first.*

He looked around the room. It was dim, but he could easily make out the huddled groups. Most of them were rubbing their eyes and yawning, trying to stay awake at all costs, but a few had succumbed to their weariness and dozed away on the floor.

Brave, but stupid, SAM thought to himself. Even if he wanted to, he doubted he could fall asleep. You'd have to be mad to be able to relax after The Forgetting attacked just a few moments ago. It was the third attack since SAM had arrived, and they seemed to be happening more and more often.

The attacks always started off as a blur just on the edge of

SAM's field of vision. A smoky haze, a shadow without an owner, a winter's cloud. But this cloud moved with a purpose – a chill intelligence – and would snake through the room with an unnatural quietness, seeming to be on a search for something.

What it was looking for, SAM couldn't quite figure out. But when it made contact with someone . . . SAM shuddered at the thought. If someone so much as brushed up against the darkly weaving cloud, he or she would vanish in a burst of deafening silence, exploding into a vacuum of time and space. It was as if they were completely *forgotten*, with little memory of their existence left behind.

If SAM could have escaped the room, he would have done, in a heartbeat, but it was as devoid of windows and doors and any sort of escape as it had been when SAM had first woken up there.

Like everyone else, SAM had no recollection of where he'd come from. All he knew was that this room was someone's brain, and he was a message. A thought. A brief moment of consciousness. A piece of knowledge or an idea that the brain's owner had picked up that day.

So was everyone else in the room. However, with every attack by The Forgetting, the room grew emptier and emptier, but there were still quite a few other messages like him. Big thoughts and little thoughts. Tall messages and short messages. Quiet thoughts and loud, brash thoughts that tried pounding and punching on the walls of the room to figure out what was happening to them. SAM wondered where they'd all come from. Were they as scared as he was?

"Pssssst!"

The noise startled SAM out of his thoughts. He turned and almost bumped into Dick. Dick was a whirlwind of a message. The two had met each other when The Forgetting first started attacking, and they'd been inseparable ever since.

"I just overheard some other messages talking," Dick said. He looked around and leaned in closer. "Apparently, there's a secret to surviving and protecting yourself from The Forgetting."
"What?!" All thoughts of tiredness and exhaustion evaporated from SAM's mind. "Where? Who? What did you learn?"

"There's a rumour that some messages didn't just survive all of the attacks. Some say, they actually unlocked the purpose of this room using three Rs."

"Oars?"

"No, 'R.' The letter!" Dick traced a letter "R" figure in the air with his finger. "They're saying that each 'R' represents a powerful secret." Dick's voice dropped to a whisper. "All I know is that the first 'R' is 'REDUCE.' If we –"

Dick stopped midsentence, his eyes widening. "Don't. Move." Dick's voice was uncharacteristically low, and SAM immediately knew what was happening.
SAM glanced down and saw his feet surrounded by swirls of

dark fog, writhing like vipers. A tentacle of fog reached up toward his face.

That's when the adrenaline kicked in. SAM held his breath, squeezed his eyes shut and ran. A tentacle of fog reached toward him and he dodged, bending backward and breezing past it. He felt light and full of energy. Another twist, another turn and he was clear.

SAM collapsed to the ground, his knees shaking and his arms gelatinous. Dick knelt at his side, the concerned look on his face obvious. "Are you okay?" Dick asked.

"I think so," SAM nodded. His breath slowly returned to his chest in heavy pants. *"This is insane!"*, SAM thought. It was the first time that The Forgetting had been this close to someone and not finished the act. "What happened? Why didn't The Forgetting take me?"

"Maybe it's because you're unforgettable," Dick laughed, the joke hanging awkwardly in the air after such a tense moment. "Hey, come with me," Dick said. "I made a couple of new friends today, and they might be able to help us uncover more about the three Rs. We don't want any more close calls like that."

SAM agreed. *"That was way too close for comfort,"* he told himself. *"If there's something to this 3R rumor, I will find it if it's the last thing I do."*

REDUCE Your Information to a MESSAGE
...because everything else is just noise

"Wait a second," you're probably thinking. "What's happening to SAM?" This feisty little message is on the brink of discovering the secret to surviving. Everything hangs in the balance as SAM tries to survive attacks by The Forgetting and avoid being forgotten and erased. In this section, we'll explore and explain some of the things that are going on behind the scenes so you can understand the power and impact of what's happening to SAM and how that relates to your own message and communication!

As Dick was just starting to explain before SAM had his brush with The Forgetting, thoughts and messages have a better chance of surviving in the brain if they've been **reduced** to a core, specific, succinct **message**. Everything else is just useless **information**, useless **noise**.

Every day, our brains are inundated with information. We collect and then discard it as quickly as we receive it. For something to be truly memorable, the sender of a message — that's you, whether you're a public speaker, author, writer, movie director, loving parent, concerned friend or anyone else with a message — must boil all that information down to its core essence.

Think of a gold panner. Her pan is full of dirt and gravel and rocks. All that stuff is **information,** but when she sifts through it and gets rid of all the extra content, the flakes of gold — the most important thing in the pan — is what's left and she saves it and treasures it. That's the difference between **information** and **message**.

If SAM and Dick had watched closely, they would have seen that the messages who couldn't outrun The Forgetting were those that were bogged down with backpacks, briefcases and boxes of information. The sender of these messages hadn't reduced them, and all this baggage content weighed them down and they were the first to go.

But when a message was **reduced** and very focused in purpose and intent, it was agile and quick and could better outrun The Forgetting. However, one can only run for so long, so it's not the only key to long-term survival, but it's an important start to building or strengthening a desired mindset!

While these messages don't know where they each came from, the person who made the surviving messages did a good job taking the source material — whether it's a book or a movie or a conference presentation or a personal lecture for your children — and asking important questions such as:

• What's my ultimate message?
• If the audience could remember one thing, what should it be?
• What is the one thing I want my audience to do after this?
• If someone successfully hears and remembers my message, what does their life look like? How do they change?

These questions can help you narrow your concept from intention (Example: "I don't want my children to do drugs") to actionable message (Example: "Don't do drugs.") There's nothing wrong with having good intentions, but a strong, powerful message takes that intention and turns it into an action-based impact line.

While boiling down content into its core, vital message is a lot of work upfront, **reducing information to its ultimate message** or messages and **focusing your intent** ensures that the person who sees, hears or reads your message has a better chance of remembering what you have to say.

🧠 Story Science: Reduce

Part of the unique format of this book is that we take complex brain science and turn it into an easy-to-follow story. And while it's presented as fiction, everything the story's characters explain is based on real research about how you can effectively and quickly craft messages that have impact and staying power. After all, you'll want to do your part as a message sender and Mindsetter to help messages survive The Forgetting so you can help your family, friends and community!

As SAM and Dick have learned, **reduction** is key. There are two core scientific purposes behind the necessity to reduce all of your information into a clear, succinct message.

First, over the past century, we have seen many scholars and researchers posit differing views on the mechanics of memory. From Théodule-Armand Ribot (1839-1916) to William James (1842-1910) to Hermann Ebbinghaus (1850-1909) to Richard Semon (1859-1918) to Donald Hebb (1904-1985), all have made significant contributions to the scientific field of memory. More recently, and with the help of new and advanced technology such as the fMRI (functional magnetic resonance imaging), many neuroscientists, psychologists and memory scholars (for example, Eric Kandel, George Miller, Daniel Schacter, John Medina, and Elizabeth Loftus) have continued to make huge gains in our understanding of how memory is believed to be encoded, stored and retrieved.

The collective research, from the vast number of the scholars noted above, leads to inference-based research suggesting that when the brain is in "intake overload" it's forced to make room in your memory banks by using what is analogous to the FIFO (First In, First Out) or LIFO (Last In, First Out) method of storage. Essentially, the messages and pieces of information that arrive in your brain first or last (depending upon the memory theory you subscribe to) are at the highest risk of being dropped (forgotten) to make room for new information. For your audience or target group, this becomes nothing more than a "hope strategy": you do a lot of talking and "hope" that your message will be remembered.

To counter this challenge, you need to ensure that you reduce your information into a clear, succinct message so that you keep your listener's brain from going into "intake overload" and forcing it to use the FIFO or LIFO method.

Second, the vast majority of memory researchers and scholars agree that the average person has the capacity to hold only seven bits of data/stimuli in their short-term/working memory bank at any one time (plus or minus two). Note, some memory scholars believe it's even less than seven (yikes). Many people refer to this as Miller's Law, named after George Miller (Princeton University) who first wrote on this topic in his seminal research paper in 1956. One can infer from this research that if your overall message contains lots and lots of data points (e.g., bits of information you wish your listener to remember), the most your listener will remember (on average) is between five and nine data points. Therefore, to optimize memory storage for easier and more accurate recall at a later date, it is imperative to reduce your information to a clear, succinct message with just a handful of data points required for maximum recall.

 # The 3Rs in Real Life: Reduce

Whether you realize it or not, CEOs, marketers, public relations experts and other message senders use the concept of reduction every day in messages they send to you. The following real-life examples show just how effective reduced messages are on your own mind and actions, and these examples can help give you inspiration about how to make the first of the three Rs work for your own messages.

Reduce in advertising:

When you read the slogan "Just Do It," what brand immediately comes to mind? Nike has been using this slogan for years to influence people effectively. When you see gold double-arches, do you recognize McDonald's? When companies create their slogans, logos or brands, they are essentially asking themselves how to take everything they do and reduce it to its ultimate core look, message or sound. It's so incredibly effective, ABC News reported that children as young as three are able to recognize and remember brands like McDonald's and Disney.

Reduce in entertainment:

TV shows and movies aren't simply a matter of pointing a camera at an actor and yelling "Action!". In fact, most of the movie magic happens in the editing room. In general, film directors will shoot at a ratio of up to 20:1. That means that up to 20 minutes of footage was shot for every minute of a TV show or movie that you actually end up seeing in the final product. In other words, your favorite two-hour movie was probably edited down from a whopping 40 hours of footage. The editor cuts and splices scenes to reduce and highlight the best of what was shot. And that makes for a more memorable TV show or movie.

Reduce in public speaking:

We live in the modern media age of the sound bite. The next time you watch the news, pay attention to the speeches and announcements made by politicians or business spokespeople. Notice how they identify and repeat specific phrases and sound bites to ensure their core message isn't lost in the noise of a long, rambling speech. Even history's most memorable speeches, like Martin Luther King, Jr., declaring "I have a dream," highlight the importance of reduction.

The 3Rs in the Authors' Words: Reduce

Throughout this book we will share with you some of our own experiences regarding how we have applied (and sometimes failed to apply) the 3R-Methodology. Our hope is that you will see just how powerful and relevant 3R-Messages really can be in a wide range of settings.

MICHAEL: "I was recently on a long flight. I like to bring books with me to help pass the time, and I picked up a book on product marketing. When I got home, I told my wife how I had just read an amazing book, but that it made me so angry. 'Why, I thought you said it was a great book?' she asked. 'It was,' I agreed. 'But what I found was that while I enjoyed reading the book, I couldn't remember any actionable items because it had too much supplementary information. The authors did not help me, the reader, to break down all the information into core messages so that I could have some real take-aways to use. By the time I got off the plane, I'd already forgotten a lot of what I'd read!' We all have experiences like that, where we say, 'Wow, that was so much to remember!' and end up remembering none of it."

WILLIAM: "As I walked off the stage after presenting my first industry keynote in front of more than 500 business executives, I was greeted by one of the audience members. She said she loved my speech, but thought it had too many 'interesting' facts. 'After your first 10 minutes of speaking, I had no idea where you were going with your presentation and what I needed to focus on,' she humbly explained. That's when I realized that she was right: I was presenting a lot of information, but that's all it was. I needed to figure out what my headline was. This was one of the best pieces of advice I ever received, and I have used it to hone and tailor my future presentations to this day!"

* A special thanks to Kare Anderson, a communication extraordinaire, for humbling me with her feedback that day!

DEREK: "My wife and I have six young children and one of our objectives in life is to build into them some core character traits. We often do this through family night discussions and activities. On one of these occasions, I was particularly excited about my message to them about patience. In my enthusiasm, I included definitions, examples of their lack of patience, admonitions about how patience can significantly improve their life and relationships, and more. Near the end of my appeal, one of my kids looked up at my wife and said, 'Mom, is dad almost finished talking about patience? I'm ready for ice cream.' Ouch! I should have seen that one coming. The good news is that I learned an important lesson about the need to reduce my message. The bonus was that I also picked up a great example for my next lesson on patience."

CHAPTER 2

Your own personal application ...

To recap Chapter 1, reduction is a key difference between "information" and "message". When looking at your own message, conduct an analysis to see if it's wrapped in extraneous information or if it can be reduced further.

For example, review the following statement: "Drugs have a lot of bad side effects and kill thousands of people every year in overdoses and medical interactions, and they also contribute to job loss, poor health, broken relationships and more."
While that message is true, it's also a lot of unnecessary information. Reducing it to its ultimate message might look something like this: "Avoid drugs if you want to live the best, healthiest and most successful version of your life."

Now, it's your turn. Copy your original message from page 17:

Copy your original message from page 17:

_____

_____

_____

What's the ultimate intent for your message? What do you want your audience/listener to do after getting your message, and if your audience could remember just one thing, what should it be?

With those questions in mind, re-write your original message to be as short as possible. The statement must be boiled down to just one core concept. Look for trigger words like "and" or "or", which may hint that you're trying to squeeze in two or more concepts into a single message.

Write down a reduced version here:

_____

_____

_____

You've just practised the first step of the first R of the 3R-Axiom. Will that be enough? SAM is about to find out...

"Nope not here"...

...Dick said for the umpteenth time. He and SAM had been scouring the crowded room looking for Dick's new friends for what felt like forever, with no luck. "I swear they were in this corner, but they probably fled somewhere else when The Forgetting attacked."

SAM ran to catch up as Dick sped ahead, moving with quick determination. The two moved with ease compared to everyone else in the room. Many of the others were carrying bags and backpacks, with a few even tugging on heavy suitcases. SAM and Dick, meanwhile, weren't burdened down, which made navigating the crowd so much easier.

"Aha!" Dick yelled. A group up ahead was waving at the two of them, and Dick broke into an excited jog toward them.

"This is Luci," Dick gestured as he began to introduce SAM to the group, rattling off name after name. "And this," he pointed, "is Igor."

"Nice to meet you," Igor said, extending a hand. SAM shook it, eyeing his new acquaintance. Igor looked neither ordinary nor extraordinary. If SAM had to define him, he would say Igor looked as boring as, well, dry toast. Not something you'd write home about. *Definitely not like someone who has all the answers,* SAM thought to himself.

"These are the ones I was telling you about," motioned Dick, who was already chatting and making small talk like he'd been friends forever with everyone in the group. "They've heard the rumour about the three Rs, too!"

"Sure have," nodded Igor. "And we're not the only ones. After the last visit from The Forgetting, we heard a few other groups talking about the second R."

SAM felt his pulse quicken and leaned forward. "We know about the first R, but everyone else we'd talked to were clueless about the rest of it!"

"If there's a clue about the 3R-Axiom, Igor can sniff it out," laughed Dick ironically. The rest of the group chuckled along. Dick flashed a smile and fist-bumped Igor with easy nonchalance. "Igor is one of the smartest in here. He's been here a little longer than us, and has been asking around about the three Rs to find out more."

SAM felt a strange feeling rising up inside. Jealousy? Anger? A bit of both? Everyone seemed okay with this situation, but nothing was okay! They were trapped in this white-walled prison, clinging to the hope of a rumour, and constantly at risk of another attack from The Forgetting. SAM knew desperation makes people think crazy thoughts, but why did he have to feel so useless? What strengths or talents could he lend? Dick seemed to have it all. What was the use?

SAM was so deep in his sulky thoughts that he didn't notice how quiet the room had grown until, while staring at his hands, he noticed the tips of his fingers were numb with cold.

"Huh?," he thought. *"What in the world..."*

SAM looked up. Something wasn't right. His eyes darted around the circle until they landed on Igor, his new acquaintance's eyes wide and mouth pursed in horror.

The group was smaller.

The circle was broken.

Someone was missing.

That someone? Dick.

SAM let out a cry and stumbled forward on hands and knees to where Dick had been sitting just a moment ago. The floor was chilled. Little frost crystals sparkled where his friend had been. No one dared speak, but SAM knew what had happened. The Forgetting.

He stood up, head spinning and fists clenched. He was about to storm off – seeking what, his confused but angry mind could not fathom – when Igor pulled him back down.

"Don't!" Igor whispered hoarsely. "The fog has moved on, but it's still here somewhere and has not yet left."

"I don't understand!" SAM said through clenched teeth. "Why Dick?"

"Why *not* Dick?" Igor replied.

"The Rs!" SAM exclaimed. "This stupid, magical axiom that everyone is just *sooooo* intent on finding – it obviously isn't true!"

"The first R, yes. Yes, you're right, Dick had the first R going for him. But there's more to it than meets the eye."

"What do you mean?"

"There's more than one '*oar*' needed to row this boat safely to shore."

"Okay, that was the worst!" laughed SAM.

Igor grinned. "Your friend – *our* friend – was on the right path, but his boldness, his complexity and his confidence were ultimately his downfall," explained Igor. "Dick was flashy and shiny, full of bravado and swagger. He was fast and kind of full of himself, like a whirlwind. His complexity caught the attention of The Forgetting, and he got tangled up with The Forgetting and couldn't outrun it."

SAM felt deflated and confused, but it was making sense. Maybe, in this twisted world, his simple nature – what he'd previously been mistaking as inadequacy and uselessness – was not a weakness, but a strength!

Igor smiled slightly as he watched SAM's face change from fear to just a hint of calm bravery. "Before I tell you what I know about the second R, I think we have to talk a bit more about the first one. There are a few things you need to know. A few bits of information I've picked up over time. Since you've survived this far, you probably know it here…" – Igor tapped SAM's chest – "but not yet here…" – Igor pointed at SAM's head.

"It's not too late," Igor said. "There's still hope for us."

SAM looked around him, the white room's stark walls reflecting in his eyes. He looked over at Igor, a new alliance already forming. "I sure hope so," SAM said.

Make your message SIMPLE

...because clarity brings focus

With the disappearance of Dick, SAM is realizing that there are no safe zones in this risky situation. The Forgetting takes no prisoners, and everyone is at risk. Even those closest to him.

At first, SAM thought the key to survival was being reduced to a core message — everything else is useless noise. While that's true, there's more to this than he realized. If we'd been able to eavesdrop on his and Igor's conversation for just a few more moments, we would have heard Igor explain more about the Achilles' heel of his lost friend.

"I am a communicator. My job is to make complex things easy to understand."

John C. Maxwell, author[8]

As you learned in the opening chapter, reducing information to a core message is the first step in delivering messages that have a long-lasting impact. However, doing this well is not just an impersonal, automated technique, but a careful art. The parameters and guidelines we use to reduce a message are just as important as reduction itself.

As Igor hinted, messages must be reduced to something **simple**. SAM, for all his self-doubt, is exactly that: simple.

Dick, on the other hand, with his energetic enthusiasm, boldness and complexity, is the opposite. He was big and full of himself and all over the place, like a stormy whirlwind of a message. In fact, if you were to break his name into an acronym, Dick would be a differentiated, impersonal, complex and kingly message.

In the real world, messages like Dick might be reduced to a core message, but the message is complicated and impersonal, often including a lot of passive third-person communication. The message is also often kingly, meaning the audience is treated as inferior to the message or the sender. In the end, the audience hears your message, but doesn't truly understand what you mean by it.

It's easy to make your message too complex. It's much harder to boil down your message to a very simple statement. Advertising slogans are a great example of messages that have been reduced to be as simple as possible. When Apple introduced its earliest computers, no one would have remembered it if it had explained itself as being, "A new computer system for cool, artistic, creative professionals." Instead of getting complicated, Apple simply went with the following slogan: "The computer for the rest of us." It alludes to the brand's outsider status and the core message of Apple, but in a very, very simple way!

It's important to note that "simple" does not mean a lack of information. Think of the *Book of Proverbs* in the Bible, or common phrases and sayings like "Two wrongs don't make a right" or "The pen is mightier than the sword." These messages are deceptively simple and extremely easy to remember, yet they each pack a lot of information with exceptional focus and clarity.

As we've already learned, **reducing information to its ultimate message** and **focusing your intent** ensures that the person who sees, hears or reads your message has a better chance of remembering what you have to say. Take it one step further to ensure your message's survival on its way to build and strengthen a mindset: make your message as **simple** as possible.

Story Science: Simple

It may be common sense that complex messages are harder to remember than simple messages, but the reason may surprise you. Many research studies have shown that simplicity is great for memory. With simplicity, it's easier for the brain to register and recall fresh stimuli (information) that's being learned. That's because the more complex a message is, the more anxious you may feel about learning it. This anxiety or fear triggers an avoidance symptom in our mind and bodies. Just as your body instinctively avoids things that cause physical pain, your brain recoils from things that cause mental anguish. Complex messages and the anxiety they create prompt a quasi-survival mode and negatively impact the brain's hippocampus, which, in turn, hinders memory storage and recall.

Many neuroscientists[9] believe that, from an evolutionary perspective, our brain has two core functions: to keep us safe and to make life as easy as possible. When making decisions, it is believed our unconscious mind will always want to take the path of least resistance. For example, let's say you're on a diet. You're hungry and open the fridge and are faced with a big piece of cheesecake. While you could drive to the store to buy something healthier, your brain will ask: "What is the easiest option?" It's no wonder that cheesecake is so tempting. We can make a literary jump and infer that easy and simple are one and the same.

We see this playing out in the approach–avoid mechanisms of the brain. If the brain views incoming stimuli as positive, rewarding and non-threatening, it triggers the reward systems of the brain, releases dopamine into our brain and fosters an "approach" (engagement) behaviour. Conversely, if the brain views incoming stimuli as threatening, negative and complex, it will trigger an "avoid" behaviour and move the brain to disengagement. Therefore, viewing this science through the lens of simplicity, making your message simple and easy to understand will better engage your participants and they will want to "approach" the information in your message. On the other hand, if your message is rooted in complexity, it could easily trigger fear and uncertainty, leading to "avoidance" behaviour from your participants and resulting in them wanting to disengage from your message. All this happens in the subconscious but has real-life impacts on learning.

To make all of this simple, remember:

The brain has an easier time registering and recalling new information that's simple. In contrast, complex messages create anxiety, and run the risk of triggering the brain's "avoidance symptom" which makes it harder for the brain to register and recall information.

 **The 3Rs in Real Life: Simple**

Some of the most memorable things in your life are surprisingly simple. Apple is often vaunted for revolutionizing personal computing, but all it really did was take a complex machine and very technical, complicated usage requirements and turn it into utter simplicity in both exterior design and everyday use. If you have an Apple iPad, you'll know that there is no way to customize its navigation and interface, and it has just one physical button. When the iPad was introduced to the public, most tablet computers were powerful but complicated devices. Today, the simple iPad has exploded in popularity.

"It's simple, but not easy!"

Walt Disney

You also see the power of simplicity in everyday communication. Throughout history, fables and proverbs taught people important concepts wrapped in short statements and pithy stories. That still happens today. Popular books sum up complex concepts into a series of short steps or simple exercises, like Stephen Covey's *7 Habits of Successful People* or Rick Warren's *The Purpose-Driven Life*.

Logos, ad slogans and products all around us are rich in meaning while being simple in essence. Applying this concept to your messages can be just as revolutionary to your communication as Apple's launch of the simple iPad.

The 3Rs in the Authors' Words: Simple

Derek: "I once witnessed a powerful example of communicating with simplicity and the art of getting your whole message across in a few well-constructed words. Australians are known for their abbreviations and catchphrases. One of those abbreviations that I love is 'ta' - shorthand for 'thank you'. While living down under a few years ago, one poignant moment brought home to me the stark realization that 'more content' does not necessarily mean 'more substance'. Growing up, I was accustomed to long and elaborate prayers at mealtimes or in church. One day, we had invited some Australian friends over for dinner. As we prepared to eat, we went around the table and each offered a prayer of thanksgiving. Most were the typical 'Dear Lord...' type prayers. When we finally came around to the last person, this wise old Australian gentleman simply bowed his head and said 'Ta pa'. With two simple words he had expressed as fitting and complete a message as anyone before him and he had taught me a powerful lesson in communicating with profound simplicity."

Michael: "As a strategy consultant and leadership coach, I typically have clients with great intellectual capacity. During strategy workshops or leadership trainings, a lot of complex models and concepts are discussed, developed and shared. The fascinating thing is that as we make decisions, one of the executives in the meeting will always call for a simple explanation for what is being discussed. 'Can someone just explain this in simple terms?' he or she will ask. It doesn't matter how complex and sophisticated the matter we discuss, and it doesn't make a difference how intellectual the audience: it all boils down to how simple and to the point can we explain something?"

William: "When I lead an executive-level coaching engagement, I leverage many tools to gather information about my client (for example, 360s, interviews, observations, and so on). I then need to take all of this data and help my client find the key themes/messages that are consistent throughout.

This requires helping them to weed through a treasure trove of information (often more than 100 data points) by trying to identify all the themes they're presenting. I then try to find the common theme, stripping out the 'noise' and focusing on just one key behaviour (message) that needs to be strengthened or developed. If I were to say, 'Here is a list of behaviours we need to focus on,' it could be overwhelming and no one would hit their goals. But if I say, 'Here's one behaviour to change this year,' we know exactly upon what to focus and it's easier to remember and accomplish. It's essentially the act of reducing a message to be as simple as possible. Simplicity works in communication, leadership and so many arenas of life and business."

CHAPTER 3

Your own personal application …

Advertising slogans are a great example of the Chapter 2 principle of reducing a message to be as simple as possible. They boil down an entire company's ethos and passion into a single statement. Taking a similar approach to your own message can help you practice this concept. Can you make your message simpler and easier to grasp for your loved one, co-worker or audience?

Write down your reduced message from Chapter 2 here:

_____

_____

If necessary, write an even simpler version of your message here:

_____

_____

Remember, your message is fighting for survival to build and strengthen a desired mindset. Don't worry if it takes you some time to get your message dialed-in to its core concept. Taking your time to get it right is not just okay, it's a great practice to hone. Everything you can do to prepare your message right now, before sending it out into the world, will better empower it to survive and thrive. As SAM is learning, he'll need all the help from you that he can get…

What in the world?...

...SAM tilted his head to the side quizzically, staring. Something had caught his attention out of the corner of his eye, and now he found himself staring at it, completely dumbfounded and confused. He had no idea how, in the entire time he'd been searching and exploring this whitewashed room, he'd missed it.

A tree.

An actual tree.

Right there in the middle of the room, tall branches stretching towards the ceiling and shimmering roots reaching deep into the white floor, pulsating with some type of glowing energy.

"Have you seen this before?" Igor asked.

SAM shook his head. "Never."

"Why is there a tree in this room?"

"No idea."

"Is it safe?"

"Let's see." SAM inched towards the tree, thoughts of The Forgetting and Dick's recent demise making him break into a nervous sweat. What if it was a trap? What if The Forgetting was testing them?

Up close, SAM realized the tree was unlike any ordinary tree. It had no leaves, and its branches looked more like oddly shaped arms. The pulsating lights made it look like the tree was moving.

"Wait a second..." Igor croaked. SAM saw it at the same time. The tree didn't *appear* like it was moving. It was *actually* moving!

"Hello," the voice boomed. SAM and Igor tumbled back, scrambling to get away.

"Did I scare you?" asked the tree.

"A – uh, well – a little," SAM stammered.

"Nothing to be afraid of," the tree replied, "I've been here a while, I should know."

"Who are you?" asked SAM.

"I'm Synapso."

"This is Igor," said SAM, "and my name is –"

"— SAM," interrupted the tree.

SAM cocked an eyebrow quizzically.

"I've been here long enough to recognize the usual visitors. I've seen your type before, SAM."

"How long have you been here?" Igor asked.

"Long enough to overhear you two talking about the 3R-Axiom a little while ago," Synapso chuckled.

SAM and Igor gave each other a knowing look.

"So you know about these secret Rs?" SAM asked.

"Know them like the back of my hand," replied Synapso. "And I also know that trouble is coming, and you're going to want to get moving."

As if on cue, a shiver ran through Igor. He looked around as the white walls seemed to grow dim, their white sheen clouding over.

"Not again!" SAM yelled, breaking into a sprint.

Igor looked to his left, then spun to his right. Cold, foggy shadows were everywhere, materializing out of the thin air. He debated running towards an open spot, then second-guessed himself and thought about running towards a nearby group to find safety in numbers.

But just these few seconds of delay were a few seconds too many. A tendril of fog hooked itself around Igor's leg and a chill shot through him like a thousand icicles. The last thing Igor would remember before vanishing was the sight of the tree towering over him, its pulsating lights flashing madly.

SAM let out a cry. He was batting 0 for 2 when it came to friends in this forsaken room.

"WHY?!" he shouted. He looked up at the tree, which appeared blurred through his angry tears. "What is going on?"

The tree named Synapso looked down at him with wise eyes that almost looked friendly. "Dakara nani," it said.

"What?"

"Dakara nani," replied Synapso. "It's a Japanese phrase that roughly translates to, 'What is the 'so what' behind the information we have.'"

"That's nonsense. Is this a game to you?" yelled SAM.

"Quite the opposite," said Synapso. "This is a matter of survival.

To survive, you need to be relevant. This Japanese phrase is asking what makes you applicable to a situation? Unfortunately, your friend Igor was simply irrelevant. Thus, he was simply *forgotten*."

SAM sat down, burdened with fear. "But Igor seemed so nice!"

"Sure," said Synapso. "Nice. General. Obvious. But messages that are nice don't stick around and are easy prey for The Forgetting."

SAM looked at the tree, letting this revelation sink in. "Don't stop!" he exclaimed. "I want to know everything you know. From the looks of it, most of us in this room don't have a lot of time left."

The tree didn't respond right away, but its pulsating lights blinked a little more rapidly.

Ensure your message is APPLICABLE
...because everything without meaning is irrelevant

Dick has become a distant memory, and Igor – a message that is implicit, general, obvious and redundant (I.G.O.R.) didn't have much of a chance against The Forgetting. After all, as SAM noticed when they first met, he was as boring and forgettable as toast. But with his new ally Synapso, SAM still might be able to figure out what it takes to survive while he's trapped in the room.

In the first two chapters, SAM learned that information must be reduced to a simple message to survive. Now, Synapso has revealed another secret: a message must be applicable and relevant to the person you're trying to reach.

Relevance and meaning are dependent on the target audience. If your target audience is made up of stay-at-home moms with children under the age of 10, how you craft your message's content, tone and visual design will be very different compared to messages aimed at an audience full of 50-year-old truck drivers. By giving your audience a message that speaks directly to their needs, preferences, desires and demographics, your audience is better able to grasp and hold onto your message.

When you're reviewing your simple, reduced message and wondering how you can best make it applicable to your audience, ask yourself a few key questions to help you narrow your focus:

- What is the ultimate purpose behind my message?

- What is my audience's purpose, life calling or passion? What problems/issues are my audience facing right now?

- How can I tailor my message to answer or serve my audience's purpose, life calling or passion? How can I give useful support for the issue/problem against which my audience is struggling at the moment?

Story Science: Applicable

According to developmental molecular biologist and author John Medina, memory is enhanced when the information you're attempting to learn has inherent meaning and purpose. He discusses these insights in his groundbreaking book, *The Brain Rules*.

Medina outlines a study[10] where he tested memory using a list of 12 words (such as tractor, green, aeroplane, apple). One control group was simply asked to count the number of vertical lines in each word. Meanwhile, the researchers asked a second control group to research and find the meaning of each word in the list.

After a few minutes had passed, the two groups were asked how many words they could remember from the list. The control group that was asked to find meaning in each word had a significantly higher memory recall rate than the first control group where members were simply asked to count vertical lines in each word. Many other studies have replicated these same results. This demonstrates how finding the purpose or meaning, indeed, applicability, in a message helps people to remember the message itself.

In his book, Medina also highlights the importance of creating what he describes as "memory handles" when encoding new pieces of information. He illustrates how memory recall is optimized when a learner creates multiple "handles"; when he or she learns something new. Think of these as handles to your front door at home – the more door handles you have, the greater the number of potential access points into your house. The same holds true for memory: the greater the number of encoding handles created at the moment of learning, the easier it becomes to access that information later.

So how do you, as a communicator, build "handles" into your message? As Medina states, the best handles are fortified when the message is strategically wrapped in content, timing and environment.

- **Content:** make sure the listener finds personal meaning in the information.

- **Timing:** the right timing is central to the encoding process. As science has validated, the more elaborately we encode information in the first few seconds or minutes, the better the chances of optimal recall later. This depends immensely on what constitutes the right timing for the target audience.

- **Environment:** Ensure the learning and memory recall occur within the same setting. The scientific belief is that environmental features that are present when learning first occurs may be encoded directly in tandem with the actual information being presented. For example, when researching optimal memory recall techniques, many studies (such as those discussed in Medina's book) have demonstrated that placing individuals back in the same environments in which the material was first learned enhances memory recall rates and accuracy. For example, if a teacher wanted to make an effort to make this last point more applicable for a student, the teacher should allow students to take their exams in the same classroom in which the material was learned rather than taking students to a special room or computer lab to administer the exams.

The 3Rs in Real Life: Applicable

Some of the greatest speeches that you remember were tailored specifically to their setting and their audience. For example, when former Apple CEO Steve Jobs gave his famous graduation speech at Stanford University, he could have tapped into the many areas of expertise he possessed. Instead, he focused his speech on the specific setting, making it about the students themselves and how they should "stay hungry, stay foolish."

Politicians are prime examples of communicators who tailor their simple messages to be as applicable as possible to a specific audience. For US president Barack Obama's re-election campaign, his team created separate ad series' honed to very specific audiences, such as Spanish-speaking Americans; women; young adults; and blue-collar workers. Each campaign had a distinct tone, unique visuals, different sound bites and a message that was specific to its audience. The team was also careful not to have any crossover in the messaging, so the audience was only getting the message[11] that was tailored to them.

Car commercials are another example. Every ad you see aims to put you, the reader or viewer, into the driver's seat. It's all about making the ad feel applicable, real and accessible to you, so you remember the emotions and desire you felt when you first experienced the ad.

In the end, relevance is critical to understanding and application. You've often seen this in your life if you think about it. As the saying goes, "When the student is ready, the teacher will appear." The reality is that the teachers and the lessons to be learned are most likely around us all of the time. The difference is in us, the student. When the student is willing to look and find relevance in the topic to their life or situation, then they are able to receive the message that is available. If you take a moment to look back in your life, you can most likely see this in action. Perhaps your parents tried to teach you a lesson over and over again, but you eventually understood it when you became a parent yourself. Maybe you received some feedback about your job performance and realized that those comments made by others in your life were perhaps closer to reality than you'd hoped them to be. Perhaps even the time and energy you're using to read this book was prompted by some presentation you have to give, or a new leadership role you have, or you simply have run out of communication options with your spouse or kids or friends and are finally "ready" to learn something new. Once a message becomes applicable to you, the message comes alive and sticks with you.

The 3Rs in the Authors' Words: Applicable

William: "It is said that one of the most common questions asked at Disney theme parks is, 'What time does the 3 o'clock parade start?' At first glance this seems like an obvious or even silly question. I would surmise some people who have been asked this question may want to respond with, 'Well, duh. It's at 3 o'clock!' Of course, in typical Disney fashion, the leadership realized that there was an underlying meaning beneath the surface of this question. Essentially, Disney found the guests were asking, 'What time does the 3 o'clock parade come to this section of the park?' By reflecting on how the question was specifically applicable to the guest, Disney cast members were able to make their response much more meaningful with an answer like, 'At this location of the park, the 3 o'clock parade passes by at 3:10 pm'. When coaching leaders on message design and delivery, I have them go through their content and ask questions like, 'What is the purpose of this presentation slide? What message do you want this slide to convey? Why do you think this slide or group of slides is *applicable* to your audience? What emotions do you want your presentation to create and what makes those emotions applicable to your audience?' All of these questions help people to tailor their message to their specific audience and contextually optimize the *applicability* of their message."

Michael: "The CEO of a large manufacturing company is a personal friend and client of mine. He would throw anyone out of a meeting who would read out loud one word or phrase from a presentation slide. He would always say, 'I can read for myself. Spare me that. Instead, tell me only what it means and what you are trying to tell me.' Anyone can read information or hear your message. Your goal as an excellent communicator who builds impact into your messages is help people find the true meaning of your message. That meaning doesn't have to be one-on-one with a single recipient. It could be you and a team, or you and the organization or company that you oversee, or even you and your family. No matter how big the group of people you're reaching with your message, the message is absolutely lost if those receiving the message don't know its true meaning for them."

Derek: "People take action and change their behaviour when they are able to connect personal meaning to the change. As an executive coach, I frequently find myself in conversation with leaders who want to spend time talking about 'what' they should be doing better or 'how' they should change the way they are leading or communicating with their organization or customers. While those conversations can be valuable, they seldom have lasting impact or result in any kind of significant change unless we also discuss 'why' making that change is meaningful and relevant to them personally. Only when they apply that action to something of meaning in their own life or profession, will it become embedded and truly engage and impact their behaviours toward the change.

For example, when I'm working with sales-people, I challenge them to ask themselves the question 'why' their offering is relevant to a particular customer. I often just get back the same empty, generic response that anyone could read in a piece of marketing material, with phrases like 'this product is cheaper' or 'this product is more efficient'. While these may be factors in someone's buying decision, people don't buy things based on general marketing reasons; they buy things for specific, and often very individual, reasons. That is why the best sales-people are less interested in 'what' a customer might need and far more interested in understanding 'why' meeting that need is significant to them. You see, once you establish a need that is really relevant to the buyer, matching an applicable solution to those needs is generally pretty easy and the buy-in is so much greater."

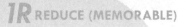

CHAPTER 4

Your own personal application ...

Knowing the purpose behind your message, and helping people to connect to that purpose, empowers your message. And vice versa. Identifying your target audience, and tailoring how you communicate your simple message to make it as applicable to their lives as possible, strengthens your message too.

It may be helpful to rewrite your core message here:

When thinking about your audience, put yourself in their shoes. Figure out what they are seeking and what they consider to be their life purpose. Then contemplate how your message is serving this audience — how it's connecting to the audience's greater purpose and answering what they're seeking.

If your message is not connecting to your audience on these levels, it's time to further refine your communication. This upfront investment of time matters for your message's survival.

You've helped SAM this far. Where will his adventure take him next?

"Tell me!"...

..."I'll tell you everything I know," said Synapso in response to SAM's demand. "In fact, a few weeks ago I found something that might interest you now."

Synapso handed SAM a piece of paper. The paper crackled as SAM unfolded it. SAM's heart jumped. The headline, in big, bold letters, seemed to scream at him:

'A SURVIVOR'S GUIDE TO THE FORGETTING'

Underneath, someone had scribbled something in messy handwriting. SAM read it aloud to Synapso.

"Here's everything you need to know about the 3R-Axiom," read SAM. "First, all information must be **reduced** to a specific message in order for the thought to survive in the brain. Everything else is just **noise**."

Synapso nodded in agreement. "Makes perfect sense," he said.

SAM kept reading, his eyes dancing from word to word. The paper explained how all messages needed to have three qualities to survive. The first was that they needed to be simple.

The second was that all messages needed to be applicable.

The third thing was…

SAM's eyes stopped as the words dropped off the edge of the torn page.

"The rest is missing!" SAM exclaimed. The unravelled paper was clearly lacking an edge, with just tattered shreds hanging where the rest of the axiom's secrets would have been revealed. "Someone's taken it, or lost it! Maybe they *stole* it, so nobody else could know the secrets of this room!"

"Don't worry, you already know more than you realize," replied Synapso. "In fact, I've been thinking. Perhaps your name itself holds one of the clues to the answer."

"My name?" SAM asked, eyebrow arched quizzically. "What do you mean?"

"In all my time here, I've come to realize that everyone's name means something. Dick, Igor – their initials hinted at their true nature. I've been writing down their personalities, and it's starting to match."

"Dick was…"

"Differentiated, impersonal, complex and kingly," replied Synapso.

"D.I.C.K." SAM's mental gears turned. "Woah. That's deep."

Synapso nodded as his friend put the pieces together. "Igor was implicit, general, obvious and redundant. I suspect your name is also relevant, or else you wouldn't have survived so long. I think your name is the secret!"

SAM glanced back down at the paper. Simple. Applicable. S.A.M.

"So what you're saying, Synapso, is that all I need to know –"

"—is what the 'M' means!" Synapso nodded. "In fact," he said. "I think I already know. I knew that whole lot, before they were attacked. One of them was Luci. And boy, was she a talker. She talked and talked, and never stopped chattering away. It made everyone's eyes glaze over as soon as she opened her mouth. She talked so long, nobody could remember what she said. She was hardly memorable."

The hair on the back of SAM's neck tingled. "Memorable!" He clapped his hands over his own mouth to try and keep the excitement in. "That's me, that's who I am. Simple. Applicable. Memorable. I'm –"

"SAM," intoned Synapso. "You, my friend, are SAM." Synapso took back the crumpled paper from SAM and glanced at it before rolling it back up into a small piece. "Unfortunately, that's all I know."

"So what do I do now? Just sit around waiting for The Forgetting?"

"No, I think that what we've pieced together so far will be enough to help us along the way to find out what the other 'Rs' in the 3R-Axiom may stand for. Are you up for it?"

"You betcha," said SAM with renewed determination.

Craft your message to be MEMORABLE
...because the way you present it makes all the difference

Congratulations, you've tackled the first R in the 3R-Axiom: REDUCE by making a message simple, applicable and memorable – just like SAM.

To recap, you can make a message simple by taking your broader communication and narrowing it down to a simple, single phrase or sentence.

Then, you must envision your audience members and ask who they are, what is relevant or meaningful to them, and how your message can connect to this deeper meaning and purpose. This makes your message applicable.

And finally, you must empower your message to be memorable. Synapso's acquaintance Luci, who was taken by The Forgetting, is the exact opposite of memorable. As Synapso told SAM, Luci chattered on and on. Her name, like SAM's name and Dick's name and Igor's name, holds significance. In Luci's case, she was long, unspecific, complicated and interesting (L.U.C.I.). She was like an origami bird: A simple sheet of paper folded into an interesting but long and complicated piece. Have you ever tried to build an origami bird after seeing one folded just once? It was probably difficult, if not impossible, because of all of its complicated steps.

Memorability is like the wrapping on a present or the packaging of a product. Great wrapping or packaging on a cheap product can make that cheap product look expensive and outstanding, while cheap wrapping on an expensive product cheapens the brand and reduces the perceived quality. Some wine makers realized this a few decades ago. By sprucing up the label and adding some gold trim, they were able to increase the price of their bottled wine by significant percentages.

How can you turn your simple, applicable phrase or sentence and make it impossible to forget? Can you wrap your sentence in alliteration, turn it into an acronym, or make it rhyme? Can you empower your message and make it even more memorable with music, a picture or a graphical image?

For example, advertisers often turn their phrases into sing-a-long jingles. The music and the rhyming don't say anything in and of themselves, and serve no purpose other than making the message memorable. These songs lodge themselves in your memory, and you can probably repeat common ad jingles that you've heard on the radio or TV with little-to-no prompting.

Other advertisers might create mental associations with something important to the recipient. For example, baby product manufacturers use babies in their logos, and warm images of mother-baby relationships in their ads, so you create a mental association between their product and the love you feel for your newborn.

In this book, one way we've tried to make improperly structured messages memorable is by turning their names into acronyms like Luci or Igor.

Consider whether you can empower your message with similar strategies to make it memorable to your loved ones, business colleagues or other audience.

🧠 Story Science: Memorable

While neuroscientists have been studying memory for hundreds of years, most of the research has been focused on how we store and retrieve information. Unfortunately, few studies have been conducted into one of the most important aspects of memory: encoding.

This is critical to the field of memory because if we cannot optimize the initial encoding process, we can't optimize our ability to ensure sustained memory recall and storage (in other words, moving the message into our long-term memory banks). If we cannot optimize storage, we reduce our ability for accurate retrieval (memory recall) at a later time.

While many neuroscientists such as Alan Braddeley, John Gardiner, Daniel Godden, and Eric Kandel have researched this topic for decades, we can have some fun and learn by going back to its origins. Aristotle wrote about several types of encoding and association when it comes to ideas. You can use them to help make your message more memorable. For example, he discussed the idea of similarity — two things are similar, but thinking of one will tend to trigger the thought of the other. For example, Aristotle wrote about how seeing a sunrise made him remember a sunset. For a speaker, this concept can have huge, positive implications on making a sound bite or key aspect of your message more memorable (for example, you can anchor two themes together in such a way that when your listener remembers one thought, they intuitively remember the other).

Aristotle also wrote about contiguity, or the idea that things or events that occur close to one another in space or time tend to be linked together in the mind. For example, when you see a waiter near you, you may think that your food is arriving.

Finally, Aristotle often discussed contrast. Seeing or remembering one thing may make you remember something completely opposite. For example, seeing the tallest person you know may trigger a memory of the shortest person you know.

Once you master ways to make your message memorable, whether it's through similarity, contiguity, contrast or other methods, it's important to understand "memory chunks". This is the number of mental groups or mental units your brain can easily store and recall. Research studies have estimated that we can best recall approximately four chunks. For example, look at the following telephone number:

16174950831

Now, look at the same number formatted like this:

1-617-495-0831

Those hyphens denote memory chunks. By breaking up information into easily recalled mental units or memory chunks, you enhance someone's ability to remember information. In other words: the better you "chunk" your message, the more memorable it gets.

 The 3Rs in Real Life: Memorable

If you've ever had a song "stuck" in your head, you're not alone. In fact, in one study[12], scientists found that more than 90% of people experience this at least once a week. This demonstrates just how powerful music, rhyming and similar techniques can be in making something so memorable; you can't forget it even if you tried.

It's no wonder that marketers have used music's ability to make messages memorable by combining slogans and commercials with earworm-like jingles. One study[13] tested customers by giving them the same marketing message twice, with the only difference being that one message was in the form of a jingle. Researchers found that adding a jingle to a message increased its memorability by more than 30%.

Some of the top jingles ever, according to media publisher AdAge[14], include the following:

"Be all that you can be." – US Army
"M'm, m'm good." – Campbell's
"I wish I was an Oscar Meyer wiener." – Oscar Meyer
"Double your pleasure, double your fun."
 – Wrigley's Doublemint Gum

But music isn't the only way to improve a message's memorability. Airlines have used custom scents[15] as part of olfactory messaging, and Apple stores are well-known for using lighting, colour palettes and more to make their store-browsing experience more memorable.

As these organizations have demonstrated, it's not enough to just have a message or a slogan. Something else must be added to make that message truly stick in the audience's mind.

The 3Rs in the Authors' Words: Memorable

Michael: "The very first training session in which I took part was a sales training programme. Decades later, I can still recall the three main messages. Since then, I've taken many other courses but I've barely been able to remember any of these other training lessons. What was the difference between that first training and these other programmes? The instructors of that first course made sure that the key concepts of the seminar were crafted in an easy-to-remember format: they were short (each of them only three words long) and they used words that would generate a clear, memorable mental picture in my head; they were easy to grasp, and more importantly, easy to recall when I needed this information. After all, what use is learning something and writing down long, complex notes, if you can't quickly pull this information from your memory bank instantaneously when you need it most? This experience impressed me so much that in my own job as a trainer and coach I am always trying to word my key messages in that fashion, because I want those messages to stick and not be lost."

William: "Years ago, I was being certified to teach a specialized programme about athletes and health. When discussing the nutrition aspects of the programme, we spent a few hours learning the ins and outs of the scientific aspects of eating for maximum energy. At the end of a programme, I was struggling to recall all the cognitive learning. Then, something magical happened: our facilitator offered to provide a recap of the learnings. She summarized with a simple phrase: 'Eat light, eat often.' She then did something even more magical: she asked us to repeat the phrase five times in unison. To this day, more than 10 years later, that simple and **memorable** phrase still rings in my head. The irony is that I can't even remember what I had for dinner last Thursday."

Derek: "I remember once asking my father what he thought were the keys to success. I was expecting a lengthy discussion and possibly even a good debate on the topic. To my surprise, he responded with one simple, yet profound statement: 'Serve others graciously.' Instantly the phrase stuck. At the time, I didn't fully understand the magnitude and impact of that thought but it has never left me and it has been lodged in my memory ever since. Whether it was the simplicity and succinct nature of his response or the fact that I could apply it immediately and often, this statement became truly memorable for me. Subsequently, over the years as I have been part of teams, led companies, started enterprises and coached other leaders, I have seen that this one simple concept has impacted every facet of my career. In fact, it is so integral to who I have become that it is now one of my core messages to pass on to my children. I hope that I am as effective in delivering it to them."

Let's summarize section 1 ...

by reducing your information to
a **Simple, Applicable** and **Memorable**
(**SAM**) Message

SECTION 2

RELATE

THE **SECOND "R"** OF THE 3R-AXIOM

Make SAM FIT...

CHAPTER 5

Your own personal application ...

The clues of the 3R-Axiom mystery are starting to come together for SAM. And for you. To survive, SAM has learned just how important it is to be simple, applicable and memorable.

Flip back to your notes and your latest draft of your message. You've succeeded in making it simple and applicable. Now, you must make it easy to memorize.

Can you change a few words in your message to make the message rhyme? Can you turn your message into an acronym, similar to how "SAM" stands for "simple, applicable and memorable"? Can you create a mental association, linking your message with something important to the recipient of your message?

Write a few drafts for your newly revised message here:

Make it rhyme:

Make an acronym:

Create a mental association with something important to the recipient:

At this point, don't worry about perfection. Give yourself the freedom to brainstorm ideas. It may take a few attempts to get this just right, but time you invest now will give your message a fighting chance. It's all up to you, as a Mindsetter and the creator of the message, to support your audience with a message that truly builds and strengthens a desired mindset.

After giving it some thought, write your newly crafted SAM message here:

This is your own personal SAM. And because you've poured so much energy, thought and planning into making him simple, applicable and memorable, your SAM message will be able to outrun The Forgetting and go on to do even more – as you'll see from SAM and his adventures.

But your job isn't over yet. As we follow SAM's journey, you'll see that your message still needs a little help from you to make an impact and to thrive, not just survive.

Something was happening...

...SAM noticed that the walls were shifting – no wait, they were opening! Little slots in the walls were slowly sliding open, and the room stirred as the other messages in the room looked up.

"What's happening?" SAM shouted to no one in particular, and no one in particular answered. Everyone was too enthralled, watching what was happening around them.

FFFWOOP.

One of the slots in the wall lit up with an orange burst of colour. Something flashed through the air. The colourful burst was actually a tiny box, whizzing and spinning at incredible speed. It zipped through the air over his head, and SAM watched in amazement as a message ran past him, leaping after the box with outstretched arms.

FFFWOOP! FFFWAP! FFFWOOP!

More bursts of colour. First a blue one, then a green one. Orange. Pink. Purple. Each colourful burst was a box, each exploding through the air so quickly that SAM's eyes could barely keep up. And rather than being directionless chaos, each box seemed destined for a specific message in the room.

SAM ran over to Synapso. He grabbed his friend's arm and shook it urgently to get his attention. "What's going on?" SAM asked, excited and concerned at the same time.

His friend motioned at the messages getting these little boxes. "Notice anything about them?"

"Not really, they all kind of look just like me," said SAM.

"Exactly. They are all simple, applicable and memorable messages," Synapso replied. "Like you, they're here for a purpose. Someone has put them – and you – here for a reason, and whatever that reason is, it happens up there!"

Synapso pointed. SAM's eyes followed and fell upon a slight groove in one of the walls, leading straight up to the ceiling. He saw more grooves, staggered like steps.

"A ladder?" asked SAM.
Synapso nodded. "A ladder to The Special Place."

SAM cocked an eyebrow. "What's so special about it?" he asked.

"I've heard rumours that it's a room where each message has a chance to make a genuine impact, but I've obviously never been up there myself," Synapso said. "Most messages haven't, either. A few have tried, but you can't make it all the way to the top without an energy boost."

"The packages…" SAM said.

"Yes, the packages," said Synapso. "Every so often, the walls open up. Someone out there is sending their messages these care packages, and each one has just the right energy boost for the message receiving it."

"And what about the other messages?" SAM asked, looking at a few huddled messages sitting on the floor under the weight of their own sadness.

"They'll be like you were before you discovered the secret behind your name," said Synapso. "They're stuck here just trying to survive, with no chance of making it up that ladder."

SAM could sense their sadness. To be stuck here, with no purpose other than sheer survival, was no way to live. He felt sorry for them, and a little sorry for himself, too.

SAM looked past the sad messages. The mood was palpably different with those who had received a colourful package. One of them was already tearing open her box. She squealed with excitement as she held up the contents in the air like a treasured trophy.

It was a bottle, filled with a glowing, neon liquid. She whipped off the cap and chugged it. As SAM watched, she appeared to grow stronger – maybe even a little bigger – as she thirstily emptied her gift.

Then, in a flash, she was at the base of the ladder etched into the wall. SAM watched her scrambling quickly up the ladder until she was just a dot, and then even the dot was too far away to see anymore.
He walked over to the base of the ladder. He put one hand into a groove, then another, but after just a few steps he was too exhausted to continue.

Am I destined to be stuck here like those other sad messages, with no way up this ladder? SAM asked himself. The thought of being stuck, and always in fear of The Forgetting, made him shudder in apprehension. SAM turned and began to make his way back to his friend Synapso.

Suddenly, SAM heard a whooshing noise right behind him. He spun around just in time for the package to ricochet off his forehead and knock him to the ground.

That'll leave a mark," Synapso said behind him.

The package thudded to the floor next to him. SAM picked it up and noticed it had his name on it, along with a big, bold label that read "2R".

"I got one, I finally got one!" SAM thought to himself. His worries and sadness – and his momentary dizziness – faded instantly. He didn't know this yet, but what was inside would make all the difference in his journey.

RELATE the message to the recipient with an EXAMPLE
...because understanding supports impact

When SAM arrived in this stark, white room, he thought he was doomed to be stuck there forever with no way out (or in). But that was only because he hadn't been in the room long enough to see that messages aren't isolated from their sender once they are sent into the room.

In fact, the sender of each SAM-styled message still has an important responsibility to help the message not just survive being forgotten, but actually thrive and make an impact.

Welcome to the second R in the 3R-Axiom: **relating** a message to the recipient with an example.

As you'll remember, the first R was reduction and was the sole work of you, the sender. The second R is a joint effort between both the sender of the message and its recipient. The sender must help the recipient **relate** to the message's subject through regular learning examples.

These examples, symbolized as a colourful energy drink in the story, empower your message to scale the memory ladder and reach The Special Place. Essentially, a learning example is an illustration of the original message that helps the recipient of your message to relate more closely to your message in new ways. It's kind of like an epiphany; a Eureka! moment; a breakthrough. Suddenly, the person who receives your message *gets it*. They understand the meaning behind the message in a more profound way, and it *clicks* mentally for them.

Think about the marketing team for a specific product. Their message? "Buy this widget because it accomplishes a specific task." They then package up this message into different examples, illustrations or episodes – a print ad in a newspaper, a commercial on a radio broadcast or a flashy special on television. Each example is communicating the same message, just in new ways. And every time you receive an example, the message the marketing team sent you – "Buy our widget!" – gets an energy boost.

Another example is the famous 18th century speech[16] by US politician Patrick Henry about liberty. Many of us know the famous concluding line: "Give me liberty, or give me death!" Leading up to it, Henry walked his audience through examples illustrating what was happening at the time in the Revolutionary War, and what would happen if his audience did not do something. The speech was so powerful, some historians say it changed the course of US history.

BEHIND THE SCENES — RELATE

 Story Science: Relate

Have you ever had an "Aha!" moment — a sudden burst of insight into a situation, or a solution to a problem you've been struggling with? Perhaps it came to you out of the blue during the day, or maybe you woke up in the middle of the night with total mental clarity about what you're supposed to do.

Experiences of such sudden learning and problem-solving are often catalyzed by what neuroscientists have identified as remote association centres in our brain. We are not conscious of the process, but these remote association centres are constantly searching for connections and matches between different things we see, hear and learn. When our unconscious mind finds a connection between all the things we've been absorbing mentally, it is believed that it pushes this insight or connection up into our conscious level of awareness.

It is important to note that many scholars[17] (the authors of this book included) believe the conscious mind must be quieted in order for us to recognize these insights and allow the "Aha!" moments to be pushed from our unconscious to our conscious level of awareness. Scientific theory often infers that, if the area of our brain responsible for decision-making, cognitive behaviour, judgment, analytic thinking, for instance, is too busy working and thinking about current tasks, it will be too "noisy" for our conscious to hear the insight being delivered by our association centres. This is why it is believed that many of us experience our best insights and ideas when we're sleeping. After all, it is during sleep that our mind is most often quieted, finally allowing our conscious mind the ability to take note of the insights being pushed into our conscious level of awareness.

The ability to find patterns and connect the past with the future was one of the late Steve Jobs' greatest strengths. His famous quote says it all: "Creativity is just connecting things." His ability to use previous experiences to catalyze uncanny levels of creative genius was extraordinary. In Walter Isaacson's autobiography of Steve Jobs, Isaacson recounts the countless times Jobs came up with an idea by looking through the lens of his past experiences and corporate visits, such as trips to Xerox PARC or classes he took in college. While Steve Jobs would say his success and best ideas came from his ability to "connect the dots," others would say his success and best ideas came from his ability to quiet his mind — he regularly created times of quiet and solitude, such as taking daily walks — so that his association centres could push those brilliant ideas to the level of his conscious awareness.

Bringing it back to this chapter's topic, we can use an example to help facilitate this act of building connections and matches between the things we learn. When you create an example, and the recipient of your message understands this illustration and relates it back to your original message, the remote association centres of the brain go into overdrive. Through the act of relating the example to the message, your co-worker, colleague, friend, or family member experiences an "Aha!" moment and receives that learning breakthrough that you're seeking to encourage. With an example, the brain recognizes the significance of your original message, empowering and energizing that message over and over again.

The 3Rs in Real Life: Relate

We have all seen examples, episodes or illustrations in real life. As we mentioned previously, Hollywood movie companies use the concept of episodes regularly. For the launch of a movie, the movie company will use various mediums to serve as individual examples and illustrations of the overall movie. It's not uncommon for us to be bombarded with TV specials, interviews with actors, printed posters, magazine ads, audio-only radio spots and more. Each example illustrates yet another element of the movie, and keeps us constantly relating to the movie's title or main message.

Or, think back to when you were a young child. When the teacher wanted to impart a specific lesson, he or she would give you the overall lesson – the message – but then use various formats – or examples – to help you relate and apply that message, to provide context. For example, your teacher may have used sing-along songs, dances, colouring projects, crafts and games to keep you engaged with the message over the course of days or weeks.

You see, it's not just about building a message. It's also about pulling the recipient of your message into the process, encouraging your loved one, friend or colleague to go beyond simply memorizing, but truly relating to, and understanding, your message.

The 3Rs in the Authors' Words: Relate

Derek: "Isn't it funny how we can often hear the same information over and over again from some-one, yet we really don't truly *hear* the message in a way that impacts us? Then one day it suddenly comes to life for us and all makes sense. Some life circumstance, pressing need or situation suddenly gives the message relevance and helps us finally relate to the message and truly *get it*. However, instead of waiting for time or life circumstances to change, I have found that a well-crafted episode or example can often accomplish the same result faster. For years, I have watched my father share a very personal story as a way to communicate why we should focus on helping those around us.

When my father was a young farm boy in North Carolina, he was shy and had a speech problem. He was in the local 4H club[18] and Mr Green, the county's 4H agent, asked him to give a presentation on pigs at the county fair. My father resisted greatly, but Mr Green believed in him and committed to come by each week for several months to work with him. When the big day arrived, my dad gave his presentation and received a second-place ribbon. After this, his confidence soared and he went on tackle new challenges in his life. "Decades later, my father had the opportunity to go back and thank Mr Green for the profound impact he had had on his life. Mr Green asked my dad what he had gone on to do with his life. My father told him that he had been a Navy pilot, a sales executive, and was now a professional public speaker. Mr Green simply smiled and commented, 'Well, I guess that little speech didn't hurt you too much!' "My father uses this story as an example to reinforce his message that 'people should use their time and lives to encourage and impact those around them.' As an example, it's personal, short, and really focuses on one simple concept of his overall message. Instantly, audiences see the direct impact they can have on a life. People are often moved to tears as they think of their own Mr Green stories and feel the challenge to be a Mr Green to others."

Michael: "I travel a lot, and over the course of the year I spend days and days in airports. I regularly hear a message that we have all heard if we've ever travelled by air: 'never leave your luggage unattended'. I have probably heard this message a thousand times. However, for the longest time, it was lying dormant in my mind. I was not consciously aware of that message and I was not really applying it to my life either. Even though I've heard the message repeated over and over again, that didn't mean I necessarily spent more time watching my luggage. That's because even though the message is simple, applicable and memorable, thus fulfilling the SAM qualities of 1R, it had never been illustrated to me with an example. It was just a monotone voice repeating the same message over and over again in different airports. If I could have related to the message through an example that illustrated the message's impact, such as a film about someone having their luggage stolen, or someone sharing their personal story of luggage being mishandled, I'd probably have done more to put the message into action. But without an example, it was just a message. That all changed the day my luggage actually got stolen! That day was a fairly dramatic illustration and one I would have liked to have been spared of. But since that day that message definetely has a very relevant and vibrant meaning for me."

William: "Not long ago, I was teaching a leadership course in London focused on the importance of humanizing leaders. One of the main concepts that I wanted to convey was the significance of emotional leadership. This style of leadership is powerful when understood and activated, but it can be difficult for some people to grasp. A big, muscular fire captain raised his hand and politely told me that he didn't agree with my message that leaders must be authentically emotional and open with their emotions. Here was a decorated veteran who had a true servant's heart, but he just could not relate to my message. And then I realized, I had an episode that could really help him relate to what I was trying to communicate.

I took him and the rest of the audience back to the morning of September 11, 2001. It was 9:30am EST and I was in a large conference room with other senior leaders from my company. The World Trade Center towers in New York had just fallen and we were frantically trying to reach co-workers who had been working in these two buildings. As senior leaders, we knew in our head and hearts it was our moment to role model mental toughness and mental grit, as all of our employees' eyes were upon us. However, there was no denying the numbness – the emotional pain and fear inside all of us that morning.

And then it happened. Our fearless leader went silent, slowly circled the room and made eye contact with each one of us, one by one. The awkward silence was deafening. And after what felt like an eternity, a tear streamed down his face. No words, no movement, just a single tear rolling down the face of one of the most remarkable leaders I have ever worked with. That first tear became a watershed of released emotions for all of us. There was not a leader in that room — no matter how tough, no matter how mentally strong — that did not shed a tear that day.

You see, our leader, through his gift of one tear, gave us permission and space to be human, to leave our mental toughness and grit at the door and grieve for those that we knew in our hearts would never be going home to their loved ones. As I fought back my own tears while retelling and reliving the story to my workshop attendees, this burly fire captain proceeded to wipe a tear from his eye and humbly stated in front of the entire class: 'Thank you for teaching me that sometimes leaders need to cry first.'

This was my *message*, and he finally got it! But only because the example illustrated the message in a new way and helped him connect to the message on a personal level."

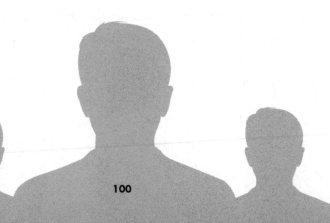

CHAPTER 6

2R

Your own personal application ...

Up until now, SAM has been focused on who he is and his own innate qualities that are helping him to survive. But when you're sharing an important message with a loved one, friend or business colleague, you don't just want your message to survive. You want it to take root and thrive and make a truly lasting impact, don't you?

That's where the twist in the tale comes. As the sender of your own SAM-styled message, it's important for you to build your message with certain innate qualities, just like SAM's sender did for him. But to energize your message to make an impact, you then have to help your friend, colleague or family member to relate back on your message with an example. As they reflect on your message's concepts in new ways through an example or illustration of your message, your message is strengthened to make an impact.

What are some examples and illustrations of your message? Think of a way to help someone relate back to your message, and write your idea here:

_____

_____

This is 2R, the second R in the 3R-Axiom. Now, will the energy drink SAM just received be enough for him to scale the ladder?

SAM tore through his package's wrapping...

...This could be his way out of the room, a chance to make sense of all that was happening to him and his friends.

SAM's thoughts flickered back to his former companions. Dick, his whirlwind of a friend. Igor, stale like toast. Luci, and all her complexities. The many others who had been taken by The Forgetting. It seemed so long ago, and SAM felt himself missing their company. If only they'd made it this far, he knew they'd be excited for him. If their sender had only prepared them better, maybe his old friends would be sitting here next to him opening their very own packages!

But no, SAM told himself, he couldn't dwell too much on the past. The future – that was the key to everything.

SAM tore open the box, exposing a small purple bottle. On the bottle's cap was stamped the symbol, "2R".

"Looks like whoever sent you here has also sent you an energy boost!" said Synapso.

SAM gleamed with anticipation. "So with this, I can get up there?" he pointed to the endless ladder in the wall.

"Yes, but only if… "

A loud crash behind SAM made him spin around in surprise. At the base of the ladder were a few messages like him, all tangled in a heap of arms and legs. At the top of the pile was the message he'd just seen climb the ladder a few moments ago. He ran over and helped her up, her hair a mess and her eyes slightly dazed.

"Are you okay?" he asked.

She wrenched her hand out of his and stood up on her own, glaring up the ladder. "I almost made it!" she groaned.

"What happened?" asked SAM.

"I only had a few more steps, but my energy gave up and I just couldn't hold on any longer."

"Just a few more steps?"
"The door to The Special Place! I could see it, and I could almost

touch it. The steps…my legs felt like jelly, and I slipped and…"

And you took down everyone else on the ladder below you, thought SAM to himself, looking at all the other messages untangling themselves at the base of the ladder.

"My name is SAM," he introduced himself.

"Sammy," she replied.

"Nice to meet you, and this is Synapso!" SAM motioned to his tree-like friend behind him. Synapso's network of lights twinkled in response.

"Did you get an energy boost?" asked Sammy. SAM nodded and pulled the bottle out of his pocket.

"Will it be stronger than mine?" asked Sammy. "Enough to get you to the top?"

SAM shrugged and looked at Synapso. "It all depends on the person who sent that here to you," said Synapso. "If the right formula is in there, it will be enough to get you to The Special Place and make an impact. And if it isn't…"

SAM didn't wait to hear the rest. He twisted off the bottle's cap.

"Well, there's only one way to find out if this '2R' bottle has what I need to get up there," he said, mustering up every ounce of bravery in his body. Part of him was worried that he'd drink the potion and be disappointed and let down, but he pushed those worries away and raised the bottle to his lips.

The purple liquid tingled his taste buds. He felt warm and cold at the same time, and his whole body seemed to vibrate. Colours popped more vibrantly, and all of a sudden the ladder seemed to loom into his vision, pulsing with some unseen light.

Without wasting a second, SAM stuffed the empty 2R bottle and its box into his backpack and reached out for the first step in the ladder.

"Good luck," he heard Synapso say behind him, but he was already halfway up the ladder and didn't look back. SAM was energized and free. He was outrunning The Forgetting, outrunning his past, outrunning the sad memories of his long-lost friends. He just hoped it would all be worth it when he reached the top.

Ensure that the example is FIT (Focused, Inspiring and Tangible)

...because it helps your audience to own the message

The myriad messages fighting for survival in someone's mind can be strengthened with an example – an illustration or episode of the message itself – that will help the message's recipient to relate to, and thus better understand, the message.

But just as a message must be carefully constructed to be simple, applicable and memorable, the example must also be carefully formulated. Sure, a poorly created example is better than nothing, but you're here to see your messages succeed at making an impact. It's crucial that you invest time into formulating just the right example – the perfect recipe for your message's vital energy drink.

SAM's new friend Sammy got an energy drink, but it was missing one or more important components. It helped her scale the ladder, but wasn't enough to get her to the top. Hopefully, SAM's sender threw all the necessary ingredients into his energy drink! Will he make it, or will he stumble and fall? We'll catch up with SAM and see the outcome in the next chapter.

What are the perfect ingredients in a delicious 2R energy drink for your own important message? Every example should be:

Focused. The example drills down to one important concept or element in your message and keeps it short. Your example must be quick and succinct, especially since many of your friends, family and co-workers are busy and don't have a lot of free time. Movie trailers are a great example of this — the trailer condenses an entire movie to just a few quick minutes. The trailer is a mini-example of the movie's overall message.

Inspiring. Research shows that positive, inspiring emotions help to drive learning, memory and impact. Your friends, co-workers or loved ones must feel inspired as they experience the example. Think back on a memorable speech that has inspired you, whether it's one you've experienced in real life or a speech you've heard online or read in a book. The ones that inspire you are the ones that stick in your memory.

Tangible. The example needs to connect with your loved ones, business colleagues or friends in a real way. Emotions, memories and impactful discoveries are triggered when someone can connect what they're reading, seeing or hearing to a real, tangible situation or idea. If it's too abstract, the power of the example gets lost and the energy drink you send to your thirsty message fizzles and goes flat. Keep it real and tangible.

Just as a message needs to be SAM-styled, your example needs to be **F**ocused, **I**nspiring and **T**angible — in other words: a FIT example. When sent to SAM, a FIT example will make him, well, fit for his adventure!

🧠 Story Science: FIT Examples

Decades of research[19] have shown just how powerful an example can be when it's focused, inspiring and tangible.

If you flip back to page 43 about the importance of keeping a message simple, a similar concept applies to examples. If your example contains too many unnecessary details – a form of mental clutter – the recipient of your example will have a harder time retaining this information. Keeping things focused and dialed-in helps to limit unnecessary distracting details and information, optimizing the brain's ability to really lay down strong memory traces for optimal recall later.

Years of research[20] also supports the notion that enhanced information processing, optimal memory storage and recall and superior learning kicks in when the brain is having fun and the person is feeling inspired. Inspiration and other positive emotions improve cognition, neuronal connections in the brain and engagement, and it leads to more "Aha!" moments and significant learning breakthroughs. In contrast, negative emotions – boredom, a lack of inspiration, and so on – creates stress and anxiety, which hamper the brain's ability to process information.

Finally, when an example is tangible and your recipient is able to make meaningful connections and take ownership of the information, it enriches association points in the brain and puts the brain's hippocampus into high-activation mode. This serves to catalyze optimal memory storage and recall.

When all three scientific elements are combined, the example is a powerful way for the brain of your recipient (e.g., your loved one, colleague or friend) to truly connect with your message.

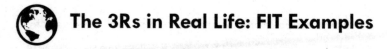

The 3Rs in Real Life: FIT Examples

Sports commercials use the concept of "focused, inspiring and tangible" exceptionally well. Brands like Gatorade, Nike, Underarmor (to name but a few) combine all three elements to create extremely popular advertisements. For example, they tend to include three major things:

- A very strong, but focused, message, such as "Just Do It". An inspiring feeling with roaring anthems, slow-motion athletic montages and dramatic, wide-angle camera angles. They want you to watch it and feel like yes, you can do it. An ending that features a product shot or celebrity athlete endorsement, promising you that you can have this — this is a tangible, real result you could achieve with your own body and health — if you use their specific sports products or gear.

- Self-help groups like Alcoholics Anonymous also use personal "examples" — people sharing their stories every week — to empower a specific message of health and recovery. Devotionals and self-help books, such as Jack Canfield's *Chicken Soup for the Soul* series, also have achieved worldwide success because they combine a specific message with a tangible story.

- Famous speeches, such as Winston Churchill's famous 1941 speech about never giving up, or Martin Luther King's "I have a dream" speech also weave focused advice with inspiring personal anecdotes and tangible action items. Or, think about parables used by Aesop, Buddha, Jesus and others throughout history. These focused, inspiring and tangible stories have outlasted their authors and continue to inspire us all.

You walk away feeling inspired to do something new, knowing exactly what that new thing is and feeling inspired through someone else's story of doing the exact same thing.

The 3Rs in the Authors' Words: FIT Examples

William: "As a multi-faith ordained chaplain, I often work with individuals who are experiencing major trauma in their lives. In my pursuit of helping others to bounce back positively from adversity and fortifying enhanced levels of psychological resiliency, I often lead with a question. I ask them to identify the one thing that is causing them the most emotional pain from the adversity or trauma they are currently experiencing. I then work to help them overcome this single pain point through a multiplicity of strategies and tactics. The one tactic I rely upon the most to help individuals bounce back from adversity, especially when he or she is feeling hopeless and not wanting to fight the situation anymore, is the use of examples/stories. These help him or her find hope in their situation and build the innate dopamine-driven motivation and courage to fight the upcoming 'fight of their life'.

When applicable to the situation, one such example/story I tell is about a 32-year-old mother of three young children. The mother — I like to call her Faith to protect her identity — tragically lost her eyesight due to a freak accident. Faith's *one* emotional pain point was the heart-breaking reality that she would never, *ever* be able to see her kids again. After a few months of working through the emotional and physical pain of her loss of sight, I was both humbled and privileged when Faith came to me one day and said, 'How blessed I am to wake up every day to *hear* the beautiful sound of my kids calling my name, something most parents will never learn to hear!'

I can't begin to tell you how many times I've told Faith's story only to have others, who are experiencing major emotional adversity in their life, realize that her journey is, indeed, their journey as well. Why is this example/story so impactful for those who are all out of hope and all out of fight? Simply put, it always FITs the situation at hand. Remember the FIT acronym?

Faith's story is **focused** because it's easy and simple to understand, and exemplifies the need to focus on one obstacle at a time. It's also **inspiring**, as her journey gives us hope, the strength and courage to fight, and acts as a beacon to guide our heart to the shores of gratitude — all necessary ingredients for enhanced levels of resilience. Finally, it's **tangible** and connects easily to our own fears, emotions and hardships, especially for parents. Hence, it is easy to feel, see and touch Faith's pain and inspiring journey to find beauty in her children's voices!"

Derek: "When trying to convey to my audiences the message that eye contact in personal communication is significant, I often share a simple FIT example about the power of non-verbal communication that I have learned from my children.

When they are very young, I like to carry them on my shoulders. After some time, I always feel a hand come down the side of my face, grab my chin and pull my face around to the side. Then a little nose comes down and presses against my nose and their eyes line up with my eyes. Without saying a word, I know my children are telling me something very specific: 'Daddy, pay attention to me!' They innately know that my eyes indicated where my attention is, and to get my attention they need to see my eyes.

As simple as it is, the power of this example never fails to connect directly with the audience. The message is focused on one specific thought — that in an era of distraction, people still inherently know that our eye contact is one of the most powerful indications of how we value people and show them attention.

It is inspiring because people can relate to it. Every parent can remember their own little one reaching out at some point to grab their face for attention. People without children can still visualize the event and directly validate the concept from observing similar situations in their life.

Finally, it is tangible because the call to action directly relates to how they have felt in conversations where people did not give them good eye contact. Or, perhaps they recognize that they have been guilty of not focusing on others when they have been talking to them. The concept is immediately applicable. They can go and practise this principle instantly with the next person they encounter."

Michael: "In my leadership training, I use a lot of personal experience to substantiate the messages that I try to relate. These personal stories help make abstract concepts plausible, tangible and understandable. Once, I was teaching the concept that you *need a goal after your goal.* I told the story of how I used to be a competitive swimmer and helped train a woman who had no lower legs. She wanted to be the first disabled woman to swim the English Channel. She was absolutely determined. This was her life goal. We tried twice – her swimming against impossible odds, and me coaching her and signalling her from a boat. Both times, she failed, missing her goal just shy of reaching land.

Years later, we reconnected. By then, she was married with new life goals. To make a long story short, she decided to try swimming the channel one last time. And this time she made it. We discovered that as much as swimming the channel was a life goal, she was unconsciously afraid of accomplishing the goal because she didn't know what to do once she achieved the pinnacle of her dreams. But now that she had new goals – a goal after her goal – she was empowered.

I used this story to help bring an abstract concept down to earth. Afterwards, an attendee said to me, 'When you told that story, it made it click for me. Since then, I have never been short of a goal after my current goal. And I keep on encouraging everyone around me to do the same.' The story was focused, since I really honed in on just one specific example in this one specific story. It was inspiring, because we all root for someone who is trying so hard to achieve success. And finally, it was tangible, since we have all been in the same shoes. We might never have tried to swim the channel, but we have experienced failure and the fear connected to it."

Let's summarize section 2 ...

by relating the message with **F**ocused,
Inspiring and **T**angible
(**FIT**) Examples

SECTION 3

REFLECT

THE **THIRD** "R" OF THE 3R-AXIOM

Make SAM FIT for LIFE...

CHAPTER 7

3R

Your own personal application ...

You've sent your friend, loved one or colleague your message. Now it's time to help them to think back on your message and relate to it for greater insight by using an example. Like an energy drink for SAM, this example keeps your colleague, friend or family member engaged with your message and it helps your message to make a true impact.

Because an example is simply another illustration of your core message, it can come in many forms so long as the example is focused, inspiring and tangible – remember our FIT acronym?

Formats for an example include a video, a slideshow, a song, a speech, a game, a fun activity and more. To illustrate, let's say your SAM-styled message is about the importance of not drinking and driving. An example could be a video dramatizing the effects of drinking and driving or a short story on the effects that drinking had in the life of someone you personally know.

Think back to the previous chapter where you wrote an example on page 103 of a new way you could communicate your message to help your family members, friends or colleagues better relate and think back upon the core concepts of your message.

Re-write that initial idea here:

Take a look at it. Is it **focused**? Does it drill down to just one important concept or element in your message? Is it **inspiring**, helping to provoke positive emotions? And finally, is it **tangible**? Does it connect with the reader or listener in a real way through a real, tangible situation or idea?

Your example sends an 2R energy drink to your message, helping it to make an impact in the brain. The question is, did SAM's sender send him the right type of energy drink that's focused, inspiring, and sufficiently tangible (FIT) to get him to the top of the ladder and enter The Special Place?

Just to help you make a quick check:

What keeps it Focused?

_____

_____

How is it Inspiring?

_____

_____

What makes it Tangible?

_____

_____

SAM had no idea how high up the ladder he was...

...He saw a faint glow up ahead. *It can't be much further*, he thought to himself, the idea propelling him forward with new determination.

As SAM scaled the top of the ladder, he found himself standing on a small platform. *Better not get too close to the edge*, SAM told himself, his feet stepping forward gingerly.

He wasn't alone at the top of the ladder. There were a couple other messages just like him. One was pounding on a door embedded in the wall.

"What's happening?" asked SAM.

The message spun around, looking surprised that someone new was on the platform.

"It took me a couple tries to get up the ladder, and I finally made it up here only to face *this*!" The message motioned angrily at the closed door.

"Is it locked?" SAM asked.

"No, I am pounding on this unlocked door for no reason," replied the message sarcastically. "Of course it's locked! It's always locked unless you have a key."

SAM's heart dropped like a free-falling elevator, right down to the pit of his stomach. *"You need a key?"*

The message gave the door one last kick, then shoved past SAM to head back down the ladder. "Hope your sender sent you a key and didn't mess up like mine did," the message snorted angrily.

SAM walked up the door.

Tap. Tap. Tap.

SAM knocked against the sides of the door, his ear pressed against its surface listening for any sign of a weak point. He pressed the lock, then kicked the lock. Nothing budged.

"Is this all for nothing?" SAM asked no one in particular. His

arms ached at the thought of having to scale back down the ladder with no new answers, no new hope. He sat down and leaned against his backpack for support when he felt the empty drink bottle.

SAM pulled open his backpack and shook it. Out rattled the empty bottle and the empty box. SAM picked up the box and inspected it. There, in the corner, something sparkled! A key. Small and metallic. Then another key. He dug through the box carefully and found four small keys, each with an "3R" logo etched into its handle.

"The axiom," SAM whispered to himself. "This is the third R!"

He scrambled to the door. The first key went in without a struggle. SAM turned it and waited. Silence echoed in response.

"Oh, c'mon!" SAM yelled, pounding the lock. He pulled the key out and tried the second one. Nothing happened. He tried the third key, but it was just as non-responsive when he gave it a twist.

At the verge of giving up, SAM tried the fourth key. It clicked when he twisted it. SAM took a startled step back as a whirring noise emanated from the door. He released the key in surprise, and it was instantly sucked in and swallowed up by the lock. If SAM had been paying attention, he would have seen the lock itself change shape, but he was too busy staring in awe as the door swung open and he was washed in warm, glowing light.

Let your audience REFLECT on the message with ACTIVITIES
...because this is the main pathway to engagement

SAM's sender had the foresight to send him not just a focused, inspiring and tangible example (illustrated as an energy drink), but also a set of keys. These keys symbolically represent the secret of the third R in the 3R-Axiom — reflecting back on the message through engaging activities.

If you remember, the first R — **reducing** a message to be SAM-styled — is solely the responsibility of you, the message's sender. The second R — **relating** the message with an example — is the shared responsibility between you and the recipient of the message. However, the recipient of the message plays a big role and responsibility in the third R — **reflecting** on the example by completing activities!

The third R of the axiom is the most important step when it comes to making impact. Real, lasting, personal impact occurs only when a recipient reflects back on the example with specific, individual activities. These activities help your family members, friends and work colleagues to apply your message's concepts to everyday work and life scenarios. You see, you don't want people just to memorize your message — you want them to work through your message, reflect on it and see how it can be practically applied. This is when transformation happens and your message impacts real life.

You've probably seen this in action yourself. After your school teacher or university professor walked you through a concept, he or she then required you to work through it with examples – visual slides, printed handouts, and so on – which were then followed by homework activities. Homework helped you to think critically and practically about the message you'd just learned, requiring you to go beyond simply repeating the message via memorization.

Examples of activities include multiple choice quizzes, open-ended questions, fill-in-the-blank statements, ranking statements in a certain order, writing a brief paragraph or even an essay, drawing an image based on a specific message, and much more.

Story Science: Reflect

Neuroscience researchers have found that when someone is asked to complete a self-reflective exercise, certain parts of the brain related to learning and memory get fired up. For example, one area of the brain that self-reflection activates is the part connecting motivation with our behaviour. This increases learning capacity, and our ability to store information and recall that same information. Thus, reflecting back on new incoming messages is essential to catalyze optimal learning, memory and behaviour, and ensure sustained impact from your message.

Starting in the late 1980s, continuing through the 1990s and surging in popularity in the 2000s, research[21] has increasingly shown that self-reflection enhances cognitive skills and learning, boosts positive emotions, encourages creativity and problem-solving, and much more.

Cumulative research[22] suggests that reflection via journaling[23] (a self-reflection exercise aimed at gaining insight into one's experiences, observations, and critical thinking) improves your capacity to become more self-aware of personal strengths and weaknesses, change your maladaptive behaviours, and even enhance your ability to relate what you are learning to your own internal belief systems and ideas (see previous chapters of this book). Most important to this book you're reading is the inference gleaned from more than two decades of research that suggests self-reflection (and reflective activities such as journaling) deepens our learning capacity and in doing so, optimizes memory storage and recall.

For example, one study had researchers tracking students in a university-level mathematics course. Students who used self-reflection journaling techniques developed their math concepts and grasped mathematical meaning much faster than students who didn't reflect back on what they'd just learned.

Caveat: Reflection techniques and strategies have long been studied as a powerful way to anchor learning. However, use that power wisely. You know your audience best. Reflection plays a powerfully beneficial role in your ability to help those with whom you're communicating to relate to, and find meaning from, your message. But for some in your audience or social circle, reflecting on certain memories, such as asking a war veteran to recall his or her wartime experiences, can create a strong visceral response. Not only is that personally troubling, but as we've learned in this book, negative emotions make learning more difficult. Thus, we encourage you to focus your audience on reflecting in a positive way.

The 3Rs in Real Life: Reflect

If you're ever turned on your TV and seen an infomercial, paid TV programming or teleshopping, or if you've ever walked past a product demonstration in a store, you've probably heard a script similar to these:

"Excuse me, have you ever struggled with dirty carpet? Try out this vacuum."

"If you hate washing dishes, you'll love this ultra-powerful dish detergent."

"Say goodbye to dirty counters. This new wipe will solve hours of cleaning in minutes."

Successful sales people know that if they encourage you to reflect on how their product solves a current situation in your life, you will be more keen to listen to their sales pitch and want their product.

Self-help services and products also work the same way. They ask you questions that prompt you to reflect on your current life and all the things you could achieve if you were happier, more successful, richer, and so on. They tie that with their service or product, and suddenly their product or service seems applicable and attractive to your current situation.

When trying to teach an important lesson, teachers make students reflect on how that lesson impacts their life and experiences. For example, if discussing why students shouldn't drink and drive, they may ask them to reflect on how injuries from drunk driving would make their friends and family feel.

The goal is to get your reader or audience to ask themselves: "What does this mean for me? How can I apply this idea to my life?" To do this effectively, be precise and focused on the individual, and avoid rhetorical questions or tasks. Your self-reflective questions or activities should make a concept or message come alive, focusing your audience's mind towards a problem or a solution, back to the past or forward into the future, inward to their own lives or outward to how their choices impact the lives around them.

👤 The 3Rs in the Authors' Words: Reflect

Michael: "I've noticed that we are surrounded by statements. But in many cases, statements are easy for us to dodge and dismiss. It's the questions that make us look inward that are usually impossible to avoid. For example, I see signs and advertisements everywhere telling people that smoking tobacco is harmful to their health.

Well, most of us already know that and even most smokers would say that this statement is true. However, too often it does not generate any behaviour change. People dodge the statement with counter statements and arguments of their own.

But if instead they are confronted with questions like, 'How does it feel to be out of breath and not able to keep up with your friends while playing sports?' 'What are you teaching your children about smoking when they watch you smoke?' 'How would your loved one feel if you passed away next year due to lung cancer?' Suddenly, these questions make people reflect on their own lives, and this type of reflection is what starts the process of behaviour change. I use similar analogies in my workshops and training to help people see the value in self-reflective activities and questions."

Derek: "I constantly challenge leaders to ask more powerful and penetrating questions. Too often, leaders are conditioned to simply give answers and directions when they're trying to influence others. Yet, the reality is that the more they give direction, the more they actually limit opportunities for people to discover, and then personally internalize, the truths the leader wants to convey.

When teaching this concept, I will rarely come right out and just tell them to ask better questions. I actually employ the power of self-reflection to make this concept jump to the forefront of their minds. First, I have them reflect on some significant message or idea that has impacted their life or behaviour in a profound way.

Then, I challenge them to consider who delivered that message and why it had such a profound impact on them. Without exception, as they discuss their thoughts, they find that the common thread is that they did not necessarily change because they were told to change. Instead, they were challenged to think differently and to work through the challenging thought or question in a personal way. They figured out what that message or behaviour would mean for them individually. Furthermore, most of them seem to discover that this personal application was accelerated when they were pushed to find the answers for themselves. As this realization sets in, another clearly emerges – that they too, need to engage others in the discovery process with powerful questions that bring understanding to life.

Through this process of self-reflection, these leaders basically teach themselves the very lesson I'm trying to convey to them."

William: "In one of my neuroscience workshops that I lead for corporate leaders, I discuss the positive impact of exhibiting gratitude and altruistic behaviours. It's one of those concepts that sound very abstract and indeed, when I layer in the various levels of brain science to support my teachings, it can become quite overwhelming for many corporate leaders. Rather than forcing my attendees to work through the cognitive teachings and science through abstract lectures alone, I rely heavily upon experiential, self-reflective exercises to aid in driving home the key insights and learnings.

It's all about creating space for them to become emotionally engaged with the learning. I use simple, but not easy, reflective exercises that require leaders to question, humbly, the frequency of their gratitude-based thinking and how often they truly exhibit altruistic behaviours at home, at work and in their communities.

Through this type of reflective exercise, leaders begin to connect the dots between the research and insights learned and what it personally means to them in practice. Most importantly, by breathing life into the learning and encouraging leaders to "dance with the data" behind the brain science being discussed, each leader has the opportunity to secure their own respective "meaning" from the insights. With that established, they can then move to self-reflection about how they may immediately begin to apply these new learnings to their current life. It really helps to bring an abstract idea to life."

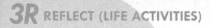

CHAPTER 8

Your own personal application ...

Now that you have an example – a new way of communicating or illustrating the core concepts of your message – ready to share with your friends and family, it's time to implement the third R of the 3R-Axiom: engaging activities.

An activity could be any type of follow-up question or homework that encourages your friends, family or work colleagues to connect with the example and apply the message in a practical manner. By connecting these dots, the recipient of your message can see how your message makes a genuine difference and this, in turn, creates changes in attitudes and behaviours.

Put yourself in the shoes of your message's recipient. The follow-up activity you use must work in his or her specific situation to help him or her connect with your example in a personal and tangible way. The possibilities are endless, ranging from simple quizzes and questions to long-form essays, fill-in-the-blank statements and more.

Copy your SAM message (1R) from Chapter four here:

_____

Write down your FIT example (2R) from Chapter 7 here:

_____

Now, brainstorm a few potential follow-up activity (3R) for
your FIT example here:

_____

_____

_____

_____

_____

Don't worry about getting it perfectly right this time around.
We'll discuss more about how to build optimal activities later
in this chapter.

SAM's skin tingled...

...maybe from the warmth in the room, or perhaps from the excitement of finally making it in here.

Here.

The Special Place.

SAM ran into the room and took a second to gather his thoughts. His head was swimming with questions and worries and excitement and fear – one big rushing swarm of it all. He took a deep breath. *"Calm down, this is what you came here to do,"* he whispered to himself.

The whole room glowed. SAM walked to the centre of the room. It dipped slightly in the middle. He touched the indentation out of curiosity. SAM heard the same whirring sound that he'd heard when the door swung open. The indentation rose in response to his touch, rising and rising as a glowing, shining tower until it was almost at a level with SAM's face.

In the middle of the tower was a button, and SAM's finger itched at the sight of it.

To push or not to push, he asked himself. There really seemed to be only one answer.

SAM reached out. The button felt hot and glowed hotter. SAM pressed, and he felt that warmth zap through his body.

The room pulsated.

It seemed to explode all around him in a burst of lights.

In the light he saw the faces of his old friends and his new friends. He felt every emotion he'd ever felt – the terror of The Forgetting, the hope Synapso always seemed to give him, the kindness of those he'd met along the journey.

And then he felt happiness. With every explosion of colourful light, every burst of magical firework, SAM felt a surge of excitement and giddiness and joy coursing through his body.

All of a sudden, he felt his feet leave the floor. Or perhaps the floor left him. He couldn't tell, because now he was spinning in the air as if he were on a wild rollercoaster ride.

"Whoooooooo!" SAM yelled until he had no breath left. The lights and fireworks seemed to carry him up and around, swarming and flittering around him in rocketing bursts of heat and colour.

Then it all went dark.

"SAM," the voice said. "SAM."

The voice grew a little louder, a little more urgent.

"SAM!"

SAM opened his eyes. He was back in the white room, the infinite ladder rising above him into the ether, and all around him were flashing lights. He realized the lights were like fireworks, exploding endlessly in the air above, followed by the "*oohs*" and "*aahs*" of the other messages in the room as they watched the airborne spectacle.

"How are you feeling, SAM?" The voice was back, and SAM turned and saw it was Sammy.

"Good," said SAM. He rubbed his head. "What happened?"

"The fireworks brought you down," Sammy said, pointing. "A hidden elevator or something – we couldn't see 'cause it was so bright!"

SAM looked up, watching the bursts of neon fire above him.

"Amazing job, SAM," he heard Synapso say. "You've done it! You've made an impact and fulfilled your purpose!"

"Yes!" exclaimed SAM. "I have accomplished my goal! I'm... done."

SAM let the idea sink in. "Wait...I'm done?"

Amid the cheering from the crowd around him, a sense of sadness crept through. SAM felt almost disappointed that this whole adventure was over. As the others excitedly talked about the message who had finally climbed to the ladder's top and made an impact, SAM snuck away unnoticed.

Design Lively, Interactive, Familiar and Envisioning (LIFE) activities

...because personal associations catalyze personal transformation

SAM finally made it to The Special Place, empowered by an example (the 2R energy drink) and its corresponding 3R self-reflection activities (the keys that came with his energy drink). Once inside The Special Place, SAM's mission climaxed with pushing the button. He made an impact, and the firestorm of fireworks is what happens in your brain when your empowered message hits the reward centres in your brain, which in turn releases a flood of the reward-related hormone dopamine — exploding with a course of hormones flooding your system like colourful fireworks.

But as you noticed in Chapter 7, SAM's package came with several keys. Each key represented an activity, but only one of them worked. That's because, just as a message needs to be set up a specific way, and an example needs to be constructed a certain way, an activity must also be built in a very exact manner that helps the message unlock access into someone's learning.

Each activity must be **lively,** because an energetic, positive experience enhances the recipient's attention and better supports learning. The activity needs to be **interactive,** because interacting with a concept helps anchor the concept in our long-term memory. The activity should also feel **familiar** to your audience, helping them to associate personally with what you're trying to do as that is the catalyst of personal transformation. Finally, the activity should be **envisioning** – when doing the activity, the recipient must be able to envision a mental image or scenario to help make the activity real to them.

Spelled out, this creates the acronym LIFE. These LIFE activities bring the activity, well, to life! When taking part in the activity, the recipient can connect the activity to their day-to-day life to see how the specific message plays a role in everything they do. This is literally the key to practical application. And armed with LIFE activities, your SAM message can unlock the part of the brain that is responsible for change, transformation and true learning.

Here are some general tips:
- Don't overwhelm your audience. Only include a maximum of five activities or questions per example. Each activity or question should have a very clear target, goal or answer
- If you're using multiple activities, each one should be different to allow your audience to explore the message from a different perspective

 **Story Science: LIFE Activities**

Activities have been shown to help anchor new information and new learning in our memory. By helping people connect to the information in new, personal ways, we employ similar strategies from the earlier chapters about making things memorable.

Research has shown the crucial importance of keeping self-reflective activities **lively** and **interactive**. Essentially, when your loved one, friend or colleague is personally interacting with your activity, it brings them fully into the present moment to focus and dial-in on what you're saying. Being in the "here and now" fully engages them in the learning moment and leads to higher levels of engagement that's so central to the reflection exercise being undertaken.

A lot of brain-based research[24] supports the notion that lively and interactive reflection exercises serve to guide a learned message into the recipient's higher levels of conscious awareness. In doing so, this helps the recipient link the message to the brain circuits responsible for personal awareness. This linkage serves to stimulate the brain's emotional circuits better and can thus lead to enhanced levels of meaning-making and more transformative – and more sustained – learning and memory storage and recall.

Similar brain research[25] supports the theory that memory storage and recall is diminished by distraction and a lack of engagement in the moment, further validating the importance of lively and interactive exercises.

Studies[26] have validated time and again that the average brain excels at finding patterns/matches and at deducing "meaning" from an event. In contrast, our brains have a harder time with a continuous flow of new information or details. Thus, if we want a message to make an impact and stick, we need to make it easier for the recipient of your message to "connect the dots" and find patterns, meaning and **familiarity** within what you're saying.

As for the last part of the LIFE acronym, **envisioning**, several decades of research have been conducted to understand more clearly the impact and purpose of mental imagery (envisioning yourself, envisioning your future, envisioning a specific outcome, and so on). The vast majority of this research has inferred a great deal of positive benefits, including enhanced levels of emotional regulation, self-leadership, goal achievement and building habitual routines, and excellence in habit formation and execution.

The ability to envision (picture something mentally) will play a key role in your ability to allow the recipient of the message to make meaning of the message via a picture in their mind (for example, a picture of something they just learned). It also helps your friend, colleague, family member or audience to project their ideas forward so they can begin to envision the actual execution of the desired behaviour coming from the message. By providing your recipient with the opportunity to see and touch the future, you help to breathe life into the message you're delivering.

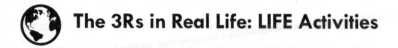

The 3Rs in Real Life: LIFE Activities

Lively

Lively activities and questions are a core curriculum component for many schools. For example, foreign language classes may have students role-playing a scenario, such as navigating a city or buying fruit. Instead of the abstract concepts faced when students simply study a book, an immersive, interactive experience accelerates how quickly someone grasps a difficult concept such as a foreign language. It brings them into the present moment to engage actively with what they're learning.

Interactive

LS Vygotsky, an influential Soviet psychologist and founder of cultural-historical psychology, honed in on interactive learning. For example, one of Vygotsky's theories notes that higher psychological functions, such as your ability to control your attention or organize information, all begins within the context of social activities.[27] Thus, interactive educational strategies provide people with opportunities to use their communication skills, listening skills, interpersonal skills, and so on. As an example, psychologists report that encouraging student discussions in a classroom enhances learning. Simply arranging desks so that students are in a circle and facing one another has been found to improve interaction, and thus enhance learning.

Familiar

Bringing something close to home and making it feel familiar can increase its impact. For example, doctors know that simply

150

warning about the health risks of a certain disease isn't enough. Identifying risk factors in someone's life will drive them to action because suddenly the *idea* of the disease connects and matches with their life; it feels personal. For example, a doctor may say, "You're 40 years old. Did you know your risk of Disease XYZ increases at this age? Here are ways to protect yourself against this disease."

Envisioning

The brain uses the same neural networks when you envision a certain task or project, as when you actually do that task or project in real life. Mental imagery exercises can thus strengthen your real life experiences. Athletes use the power of mental imagery to great effect.[28] Coaches have their athletes envision crossing the finish line, lifting a heavier weight, and so on. They walk them through this mental imagery, and a growing body of research has found that doing so actually increases performance, motivation and final execution. For example, Olympic swimming champion Michael Phelps used mental imagery to envision his swimming stroke. He created mental images of doing the stroke perfectly, and in doing so, he fortified his actual execution of his swimming stroke when he was physically in the water.

The 3Rs in the Authors' Words: LIFE Activities

Derek: "Four of my six children are boys under the age of 13. As a dad, I feel a great passion and responsibility to begin preparing them for the joys and responsibilities of manhood. One of my favorite ways to do this is to weave powerful life lessons into seemingly unstructured spontaneous outdoor adventures.

For example, we live on the coast of North Carolina and one of our favourite things to do is to "treasure hunt" around the marsh islands outside our backdoor. As we kayak through the marsh creeks or explore the maritime forests, I will begin to create an adventure that puts them right into the heart of the storyline. For example, to teach them some fundamental survival competencies, the adventure might have us stranded from a shipwreck in the early 1700s with little to no water or food. As they scramble to catch crabs, gather oysters or pick berries, I begin to ask them questions that challenge them to grow bolder, to look past the obvious and think creatively, to take care of each other, and so on.

Ultimately, my point is to engage them in life-shaping lessons that will embed simple concepts and values early on. The way that I do it is to make sure that each of these episodes is infused with LIFE elements so that it becomes real and personal to them both in the present and also as a foundation for later growth and leadership."

William: "In Chapter 7, I shared how I leverage self-reflection examples to showcase the importance of exhibiting gratitude and altruistic behaviours. As we just learned, it should come as no surprise that I used the elements of LIFE to aid me in successfully executing my self-reflection activity. Let me break down one the activities for you regarding gratitude.

First, I ask everyone to write down the name of somebody in their life that they deem a role model. I then ask them to write a short explanation of *why* that person is their role model and specifically, how their role model has made a profound difference in their life. I then ask participants to share what they wrote with another colleague in the workshop. By discussing what they wrote out loud, a higher level of emotional engagement begins. This makes it **lively and interactive**.

After the lively and interactive activity is complete, I ask leaders if they have ever truly taken the time to thank the person they cited as their personal role model. This question, within this phase of the activity, creates a sense of **familiarity** and helps the audience to associate personally with what they are learning and doing. This, as you previously read, is vital because it is the catalyst for personal transformation. Of course, this reflective question brings leaders directly back to the concept of gratitude and *how* they can demonstrate more of it (for example, showing gratitude by thanking their role model for making a difference in their life).

Next, I ask participants to **envision** a face-to-face conversation with their role model. Specifically, I ask them to visualize and/or imagine what they would say to him or her and how they envision the conversation unfolding. This last step often creates a visceral emotional response from participants and makes this future conversation with their role model very real for them in the present moment.

My final step in this activity is biased toward action. I ask every participant to take a few minutes, right then and there, to schedule a time to have this wonderful conversation with his or her role model. This could, for example, include calling their role model or sending an email requesting time to chat. By ensuring my participants take action on the self-reflection activity they just experienced, it breathes life into the LIFE elements and makes my message come alive, quite literally.

Michael: "I am personally not a great fan of role-play in training situations. It feels a bit awkward and somewhat unreal. But no matter what I think about role-play, in some situations these LIFE activities work quite well, especially if they bring a generic, plausible but still distant concept to life. One great example is the concept of giving and receiving constructive feedback. In all the leadership courses I give, the concept of 'constructive feedback' is something with which everyone is familiar and values highly. Participants can rattle off all of the correct-sounding phrases regarding how to give and receive feedback But it's only when we go through a role-playing scenario that we really grasp how to give and receive feedback well. These types of activities are lively, interactive, familiar and help bring awareness to details and empower participants to envision specific scenarios for themselves. In other words: they breathe life into a concept that otherwise is somewhat abstract."

CHAPTER 7

Let's summarize section 3 ...

by reflecting on the message with
Lively, **I**nteractive, **F**amiliar and **E**nvisioning
(**LIFE**) Activities

SECTION 4

RE-ENGAGE

THE ON-GOING "R" OF THE
3R-AXIOM

KEEP SAM FIT for LIFE...

CHAPTER 9

3R^n

Your own personal application ...

SAM has made an impact, thanks to the activities with which his sender provided him. Similarly, you must build activities for your message, which will help your message unlock access to the brain's learning centres so the message can make an impact in the minds of your loved ones, friends, colleagues or community.

Review the follow-up activity that you wrote down in the previous chapter. Now, think back to the acronym LIFE — your activities should be lively, interactive, familiar and envisioning. When done with LIFE in mind, these activities will connect with the life of the recipient, creating true impact.

If the example activities you wrote down in the previous chapter needs some slight modification to bring it to LIFE, write the new version here:

_____

_____

_____

_____

Now, let's catch up with SAM. He slunk away from the party the last time we saw him. What is he up to now?

"Are you okay?"...

...Sammy asked, looking concerned. She'd found SAM behind the crowd in a quiet corner, sitting alone.

"What's next for me?" SAM's eyes swept the room. "I did everything, and figured out the mystery of the 3R-Axiom – 1R for **reduce**, 2R for **relate**, 3R for **reflect** – and now it's all over. The adventure is finished."

Sammy cocked an eyebrow. "Or is it?" She took SAM's hand and pulled him up from the ground. "I think you're in for a surprise!"

"What do you mean?" SAM asked.

Sammy led SAM back to the crowd, and found Synapso there amid them. The crowd hushed as SAM, the famous message who had unlocked The Special Place, walked through them to get to his friend.

Synapso looked down, a proud smile shining as his twinkling lights rapidly fired. "Is someone feeling a bit down?" Synapso asked.

"He thinks his mission and purpose is over," explained Sammy.

Synapso let out a deep, hearty laugh – the type that seems to burst out uncontrolled from a place of true mirth.

"Oh, far from it," said Synapso. "Do you know what a mindset it?" SAM shook his head.

"It's a way of thinking," explained Synapso. "It's a way of seeing the world. A perspective. A life philosophy. And it greatly determines someone's attitude."

Synapso handed SAM a notebook. Its cover was stained and worn, like it had been used many times.

"What is this?" asked SAM.

Synapso looked at Sammy and smiled. "One of the messages up there handed this to Sammy after seeing you get into The Special Place."

Sammy nodded. "He said it's a journal," she continued. "Very few messages actually get up the ladder, and even fewer ever make it into The Special Place. It's so special, so sacred – so *rare* – that successful messages have been keeping a journal of their experiences."

SAM flipped the notebook open. Different stories, different hand-writing. Each chronicling the journey of messages just like him. One of the entries was written in red. "I just learned," wrote the mystery message, "that this is just the beginning. Making an impact was just the starting point. We have to do more. We are created for more. We *are* more. We were sent here to leave a legacy!"

SAM flipped the page excitedly. "Our destiny is ahead of us. We can help form a mindset, and this is our ultimate purpose and the reason we were all sent here. The 3Rs were just the beginning. Reduce. Relate. Reflect. Now we must re-engage."
SAM glanced up at Synapso and Sammy. "So, more than just one visit to The Special Place?" asked SAM.

Synapso smiled. "Exactly. It's long-term. It's more than just once."

"How does it work?" asked SAM.

"You just keep multiplying the 3Rs," said Synapso. "It's all up to you, and your sender. If you're lucky, your sender doesn't just want you to make a one-time impact – he wants you to be a part of creating a mindset. A long-term impact."

Rather than feeling exhausted at the prospect of multiple trips up the ladder, SAM felt elated. Thrilled. Suddenly, he felt he was part of something greater than himself. A chance to change a way of thinking – build and strengthen a mindset – forever! If what Synapso said was true, SAM knew his importance in this room wasn't fading. If anything, it would grow. He would have a mission and a purpose. "How will I know if I'm supposed to be part of this, this mindset thing?" asked SAM.

"It's up to your sender," replied Synapso. "If your sender wants to do more than just make a one-time impact, if he wants to change this mind —" Synapso motioned at the room around them, "— then he'll send you more packages to re-engage that button up there."

SAM's eyes followed the ladder back up to its distant, invisible top. He tightened his fists in excitement.

"Well, have there been more packages for me?" SAM exclaimed, suddenly reinvigorated with his mission.

"Funny you should ask," said Synapso. He reached down and held up another package. The name "SAM" was emblazoned across the top in bold lettering.

A package. His package.

SAM tore into it without a second's hesitation. Inside? Another 2R energy drink, and another set of 3R keys. Sammy clapped excitedly, and SAM hoisted his backpack onto his shoulders and marched determinedly to the base of the ladder.

He grasped the first step on the ladder and hauled himself up.

Then another. And another. The ladder felt comfortable to SAM – no longer a scary, unknown path to an even scarier, unknown destination.

He had a job to do.

He had a purpose.

"To build and strengthen a mindset," SAM whispered to himself.

And if SAM's sender kept this up, who knew what kind of long-term impact a changed mindset could have!

Encourage your audience to RE-ENGAGE with your message regularly
...because this will fortify the desired mindset

All this time SAM thought we wanted our messages to make an impact. While that's technically true, a one-time moment of learning isn't enough. SAM wants more. Our message wants more. We want more.

We want our message to remain powerful and strong, helping to steer our family to make the right life choices. Helping to improve the lives of our friends. Helping to boost the learning and morale of our work colleagues. Helping to enhance our communities with core values, messages and morals.

To do this, we need more than just a one-time impact. We need to support and strengthen the mindsets of those around us.

This requires re-engagement; not so much a new R, but a multiplication of the 3R-Axiom.

In brain science and studies on learning and behaviour, it's not just important for someone to get a 3R-Axiom-enhanced message. It's crucial for that person to *re-engage* with the information that he or she has learned, over and over again. Keep in mind that this doesn't mean the message is simply repeated, but that true interaction and engagement with the message and varying examples needs to occur multiple times.

This regular, repeated exposure to information employs the spacing effect. In psychology, the spacing effect refers to a well-studied experience where humans are better able to learn and remember behaviour- and mindset-changing information when the repetitions of learning themes are administered over time.

So rather than being the $3R^n$-Axiom, it's simply the 3R-Axiom multiplied. Or $3R^n$, if you will. The goal of this multiplication of the three Rs is to ensure true memory retention, supporting practical day-to-day applications and inspiring life transformation — whatever that may look like in the lives of your family members, friends, business colleagues or community!

Story Science: Re-engage

Many of the memory scholars and researchers[29] introduced throughout this book have identified hypotheses and created models to demonstrate best practices and strategies for re-engagement and optimizing memory storage and recall (for example, Method of Loci believed to have been invented by Simonides (c.556-c.468 B.C.E.)).

While there are many models worth exploring, we have found two specific scientific models especially applicable for our 3R-Axiom model. The first strategy is the model of review, repeat and rehearse. This scientific theory suggests that the more we review, repeat and rehearse the information we are trying to remember, the better our chances of recalling that information at a later time. Therefore, every time you ask your friend, co-worker, colleague or friend to re-engage with your message via review, repeat and rehearsal techniques, you optimize the listener's memory storage potential and increase the likelihood of your message establishing a mindset.

It's important to note that you should not simply ask your audience to repeat your message over and over again, similar to the old-school method of memorizing facts or phrases (often referred to as rote memory techniques). Instead, and for optimal impact, ask your audience to repeat and rehearse the emotional aspects of your message. For example, if we want our listeners to remember the phrase, "Eat at the kitchen table," it is best to ask the listeners to find an emotional attachment to the phrase, such as asking them to recall a favorite family memory while eating at their kitchen table. By attaching emotion and meaning to content that we are purposely trying to store into our long-term memory banks, we are creating enhanced encoding strategies designed for maximum memory storage and recall potential.

The second strategy is the concept of spacing. In neuroscience research, spaced learning is not a new concept and has been validated as an effective learning tool for decades. The premise is quite simple: if we wish to optimize memory storage and recall of new learning material, an extended method of time-based learning is more valuable than trying to cram all the new information into one training or study session. Think back to your time as a school student. You probably can recall more learning points/facts from times when you studied for several weeks/months as opposed to staying up and pulling an all-nighter before an exam (often good for short-term memory recall but lacking the power to drive those learning points optimally into our long-term memory banks). For example, college students who pull all-nighters for their mid-term exams often find they have to re-learn all of the same information again for their finals. This is because the vast majority of the material learned in their cramming session was held in their working memory/short-term memory banks and hence, deleted within hours/days to allow more room for new incoming pieces of information/stimuli.

Therefore, in order to optimize this learning method, instead of an all-day conference, hour-long training sessions can be spread over the course of several weeks to optimize retention.

And, instead of asking someone to read a book in one month, ask him or her to read one chapter every few weeks for optimal retention of the book's key learnings.

So, what does spaced learning have to do with "re-engaging" your audience after you've delivered your message? Re-engaging your audience is just like the concept of spaced learning. By continually reinforcing the core components of the message over and over again, the message is strengthened and made more impactful.

Re-engagement also counteracts the effects of short-term memory loss, where we all often forget the details of new information shortly after first learning it (recall the example of the college student above). By coming into contact with your message over and over again after the initial contact, the message is strengthened.

Here's how it works: providing space (hours, days, or even weeks) between our actual message delivery and our engagement follow-up often makes learning (remembering) feel more difficult for the receiver of the message (meaning it requires a lot of effort to reconstruct the past to recall what was previously learned). As mentioned above, this is where the genius in spaced learning lies. Neuroscience research has continually validated that increased effort in memory retrieval/recall leads to enhanced levels of long-term memory storage and accurate recall rates. The more memory effort we ask our listeners to exert over a determined time interval (for example, asking listeners to recall what they learned in the previous week's training session), the higher the likelihood that our listener will accurately recall the message that we have delivered. In essence, the enhanced levels of long-term memory storage and accurate recall rates are directionally correlated to the effort given to reconstruct what we learned in the past.

Reflecting back on both the strategies discussed in this section, you will note how they interweave perfectly to create a beautifully designed "memory web" required for optimal memory encoding, recall and storage. The very act of using spaced learning and asking listeners to return to a previous learning example or learning session, not only produces the type of effort that leads to optimal memory storage, but also requires the listener to review, repeat and rehearse your message's concepts. Hence, these two strategies work in perfect harmony with each other, together leading to maximum, sustained survivability and hence, keeping SAM FIT for LIFE.

The 3Rs in Real Life: Re-engage

Re-engagement examples are all around us: Charthouse Learning, distributor of the bestselling *FISH!* book and video, uses a series of online follow-up learning prompts to keep readers re-engaged with the concepts they learned in the book. For example, readers receive 25 learning reminders with connected activities that help them re-engage with the FISH! practices they read.

* Companies harness the power of re-engagement through television ads. Playing the ads repeatedly re-engages you over and over again, broadcasting the same message through various forms (examples) to keep their message strong.

* Re-engagement is necessary for physical improvement, too. If you go to the gym just once, no long-lasting change occurs. Science shows us that our bodies need constant re-engagement through exercise to stay in top shape and to grow stronger. In fact, it takes approximately 16 workouts to see changes in muscle tone.[30]

* When teachers and professors are trying to teach a significant or important lesson, they use quizzes and other daily or weekly learning prompts to keep students re-engaged with the preliminary message. By keeping students coming back to the content again and again in preparation for quizzes, exams and essay questions, the message is strengthened.

* In email marketing, studies have found that people rarely take action after receiving just one email about a commercial prod-

uct, an activist cause or a news alert. Instead, marketers use a series of emails to re-engage the consumer over the course of several days or weeks. You'll see this in action if you peruse your email inbox. Look for emails from a specific organization and company. For example, in the days leading up to a sale, you'll see repeated emails about this sale. On the day of the sale, you might even receive a "Last chance!" email. In the busy online marketplace, re-engagement ensures the marketer's message stays at the forefront of your mind.

The 3Rs in the Authors' Words: Re-engage

William: "While working through graduate school at Harvard, my clinical courses included one based on the neuropsychology of memory. The professor, with the aim of having the students experience the content and research being taught, required weekly quizzes be undertaken. Of course, I didn't understand the purpose behind the weekly quizzes until we covered the material discussing the importance of re-engaging the brain to ensure optimal memory storage and recall. In other words, students were experientially learning that we could do much better in the final exam if we re-engaged our brains on a weekly basis via quizzes, rather than cramming for the final the day before.

Years later, I stole this page right out of my professor's playbook for my own teaching methods. Currently, many workshops and academic courses that I teach incorporate frequent quizzes or self-reflection exercises intended to re-engage the learner's mind over time. In doing so, and in the same vein as my Harvard professor, I am striving to fortify memory storage and recall through the act of re-engagement. Again, as we have learned, this is a much better evidenced-based strategy than having my audience cram the night before the end of my course or workshop."

Derek: "I have found that the re-engagement process can also be used as a form of pre-engagement. For example, I have a long-standing training and consulting relationship with a large non-profit organization here in the US. We have been training its sales team and managers for several years during large annual sales conferences. Each year, we reinforce the conference content with several weeks of follow-up training built in the 3R model. The results have been fantastic with significant performance improvements each year.

However, when planning a recent conference for them, we decided to apply the re-engagement principle in a slightly different way. Ahead of the upcoming conference, we chose to re-engage the team with some short training modules to refresh past learning. At the same time we also pre-engaged them with some new concepts for the upcoming conference.

Here is how it worked: About six weeks prior to the actual conference, we began to send them small online training modules (mindtriggers) on a weekly basis that reflected on past topics. Then, as part of each mindtrigger, we would also tie in and relate a preview of upcoming content in the context of what they had previously learned. As part of these training modules, participants were challenged to reflect on the content and provide direct, personal responses to questions about how they understood or applied the concepts in light of the skills and concepts they already knew or practised.

The results were incredible. The momentum and enthusiasm participants brought into that next conference was significantly higher than any other in the past. We also found that the retention and relevant application of past concepts greatly increased. This was also true for new concepts that were being introduced before and during the conference.

The bottom line lesson: This form of re-engagement was not just a rehash of past content with a hope that recipients would further embed it. It provided a context for re-engaging past content while establishing a new relevance for it in the upcoming training. So, pre-staging a new idea in the framework of a past idea reinforced the value and relevance of each."

Michael: "In leadership training, I used to struggle with the fact that no matter how well I delivered the material and no matter how steep the learning curve was, the forgetting curve would hit in a merciless way right after that delivery. I tried everything to change this. I modified the structure of the course, provided different learning materials (for example, visual slides, physical flash cards), reduced the amount of content and more. Through those changes I was able to increase the learning curve, but eventually the forgetting curve would still take its toll.

I finally realized that this cycle cannot be broken through just focusing on the learning curve. I needed to tackle the forgetting curve itself. Instead of leaving my students on their own after the leadership training, I created opportunities for them to re-engage with the content in bite-sized reminders of the initial learning material. After doing this, I noticed quite a change in the learning retention rate of the participants of my training, so I investigated the mechanics for changing the forgetting curve in greater detail.

The result was the creation of an online system — you'll learn more in the next chapter — that increases learning retention through regular interactive reminders. It is now an open platform to be used by trainers, authors, coaches and other learning professionals that have the desire and deep passion to ensure learning retention."

CHAPTER 10

Your own personal application ...

Let's rewind quickly. When we first started our adventures together, SAM was running in fear from The Forgetting. But then he learned 1R – **reduction** – and how he was built as a simple, applicable and memorable (SAM) message. This made him fast and nimble enough to escape his enemies.

SAM then discovered that messages just like him were getting special packages containing an example, symbolized in the story as an energy drink. He received one example that powered him to the top of the ladder because the example was built to be focused, inspiring and tangible (FIT). Such FIT examples help the recipient of a message better relate to the message. **Relate** – that was 2R.

SAM discovered the third R when he reached the top of the ladder and unlocked The Special Place with a key provided by his sender. SAM hit the button inside The Special Place and made his impact. The key symbolized activities. In the third R – **reflection** – the recipient reflects back on the message through lively, interactive, familiar and envisioning (LIFE) activities.

Together, this **makes SAM FIT for LIFE**.

But that was just the start. After understanding the mystery of the 3R-Axiom, SAM discovered it's not enough to make a one-time impact. He wanted to leave a legacy. He wanted to help create a mindset, and that's done through **re-engagement**. We're talking about a multiplication of the 3Rs, spacing out re-engaging reminders through regular repetition and employing the spacing effect to ensure long-term memory recall.

Take a look at the example and activities you've written in the previous chapters. Now, try to brainstorm five more examples with corresponding activities that repeat your message to re-engage the mind.

FIT Example: _____

    LIFE Activity: _____

    LIFE Activity: _____

    LIFE Activity: _____

FIT Example: _____

    LIFE Activity: _____

    LIFE Activity: _____

    LIFE Activity: _____

FIT Example: _____

    LIFE Activity: _____

    LIFE Activity: _____

    LIFE Activity: _____

FIT Example: _____

    LIFE Activity: _____

    LIFE Activity: _____

    LIFE Activity: _____

FIT Example: _____

    LIFE Activity: _____

    LIFE Activity: _____

    LIFE Activity: _____

Through the practice of re-engagement, employing all the acronyms you've already learned, you are building and strengthening a mindset.

It wasn't so much that SAM was thirsty, but that he was tired...

...He felt exhausted. The kind of tired that seems to creep through you, starting in your toes and working its way up your body, making your limbs feel like jelly until all you want to do is sit on the floor and wiggle around like a slug.

That's how fatigued SAM felt.

It had been a long time since he'd received a package containing an energy drink and a set of keys. He'd tried climbing the ladder without them a couple times, but all that resulted in was a death-defying fall and a lot of bumps and bruises.

The longer he went without an energy drink, the more tired he felt. It was like he was fading.

"Is there anything I can do?" SAM asked Synapso.

His friend looked down on him kindly.

"You need to wait," he replied.

"I've *been* waiting," said SAM.

Synapso nodded. "Yes, you have. And you'll need to wait a little longer. There's not much you can do, you just need to wait for your sender to provide another care package."

"What happens if I don't get another one?" asked SAM.

"Nothing," said Synapso. "Quite literally, nothing. All that hard work you've put in will disappear, and all hopes of forming a mindset fades."

"I'll just wait then," said SAM in resignation. "Wait…and hope."

Will SAM's sender realize his potential as a Mindsetter – someone who has the power to build and strengthen a mindset - and come to SAM's aid? Will this Mindsetter embrace his or her ability to make an impact, not just a fleeting impression?

Now it's your turn to become a Mindsetter
...because only you can inspire, influence and impact the people around you

SAM is stuck, waiting. He's done everything he can to make an impact, even travelling up the ladder a second time. But to stay re-engaged, SAM needs help.

He needs *your* help.

He needs the reader of this book — you! — to re-engage with the message.

You'll know by now that this book you're holding is built according to the 3R-Axiom. As you progressed through this book, you learned about simple, applicable, memorable messages — in the form of simple, applicable, memorable messages themselves! Then, we helped you to relate to the SAM messages with FIT examples and by applying them to your life and the world around you. That's the second R, relate!

And finally, we began asking you to go through practical exercises and activities to reflect back on the concepts you were learning — the third R, reflection!

In fact, this entire book is built around the foundational methodologies of the 3R-Axiom. And now we reach the Nth multiplication factor: re-engagement. As SAM learned earlier, regular re-engagement through repetition helps the recipient of a message to stay engaged with a message, thus leading to true impact and the building of a mindset.

But first, let's quickly review the journey you have taken through this book. Let's take a look at the very first chapter where you wrote down your original message. Write that original message here:

What did you learn after writing your original message?

1R (Reduce) - Make SAM

Chapter 1: You learned that you don't just want to allow new incoming information to be overridden. It's key that you **reduce** your information into a clear, succinct message so that you keep your listener's brain from going into intake overload and forced to use the FIFO or LIFO method. Also, remember, to reduce your message to a handful of data points required for maximum recall (see page 25 for more details).

Chapter 2: Remember to keep your message **simple.** The brain has an easier time registering and recalling new information that's simple. In contrast, complex messages create anxiety, and this can trigger the brain's avoidance mechanisms, which often make it harder for the brain to store and recall information (see page 43 for more details). A message like Dick (Differenciated, Impersonal, Complex and Kingly) is a whirlwind of a message and gets easily forgotten.

Chapter 3: Research has empirically shown that memory is enhanced when the information you're attempting to learn has inherent meaning and purpose. Therefore, make a point of bringing meaning and purpose to your message by making it **applicable.** And, don't forget to add those memory handles (see page 58 for more details). Because a message that looks like Igor (Implicit, General, Obivious and Redundant) lacks all the qualities needed to survive.

Chapter 4: Remember that our success in recalling information at a later time depends primarily on how the new stimuli/information was encoded when it was first received. Also, be sure to leverage optimal memory techniques to make your message **memorable** through strategies such as similarity, contiguity, contrast and chunking (see page 75 for more details). And as you saw with Luci (Long, Unspecific, Complicated and Interesting), a message that is more like an origami bird is not memorable at all.

And that sums up the first R, reduce! Reducing helps capture your audience's attention. After you learned all of the above, we asked you to rewrite your message from page 17. Let's see how your message evolved to be simple, applicable and memorable! Copy the last version of your message here:

Now, let's see what we discovered about the second R.

2R (Relate) - Make SAM FIT

Chapter 5: Remember to use an example to help facilitate the act of building connections and matches between the things we learn. When you create an example, and the recipient of your message understands this example and **relates** it back to your original message, the remote association centres of the brain go into overdrive (see page 94 for more details) and through this we can push those "Aha!" moments from our unconscious to conscious mind.

Chapter 6: Be sure your message is FIT! Keeping things **focused** and dialed-in helps to limit unnecessary distracting details and information, optimizing the brain's ability to really lay down strong memory traces for optimal recall later. **Inspiration** and other positive emotions improve cognition, neuronal connections in the brain and engagement, and leads to more "Aha!" moments and significant learning breakthroughs. Lastly, when an example is **tangible** and your recipient is able to make meaningful connections and take ownership of the information, it enriches association points in the brain and puts the brain's hippocampus into high-activation mode (see page 110 for more details).

Remember how you built out an example and took it through several rounds of revisions as you learned more and more? Write the final version of your FIT example from page 124 here:

_____

With an example, you help your audience relate to your message, and this creates true understanding and connection.

3R (Reflect) - Make SAM FIT for LIFE

Chapter 7: Recall that **reflecting** back on new incoming messages is essential for catalyzing optimal learning, memory and behaviour, and ensure sustained impact from your message. Reflection plays a powerfully beneficial role in your ability to help those with whom you're communicating to relate to, and find meaning in, your message (see page 130 for more details).

Chapter 8: Breathe LIFE into your message! Being in the present moment fully engages listeners in the learning moment and leads to higher levels of engagement that are so central to the reflection exercise being undertaken. **Lively** and **interactive** reflection exercises serve to guide a learned message into the recipient's higher levels of conscious awareness. If we want a message to make an impact and stick, we need to make it easier for the recipient of your message to connect the dots and find patterns, meaning and **familiarity** within what you're saying. Lastly, the ability to **envision** (picture something mentally) will play a key role in your ability to allow the recipient of the message to make meaning of the message via a picture in their mind (for example, a picture of something they just learned) (see page 148 for more details).

You created follow-up activities for your example. What activity did you brainstorm on page 159? Write it here:

_____

By reflecting back on your message, you initiate engagement.

3R^n (Re-engage) - KEEP SAM FIT for LIFE

Chapter 9: Re-engagement is key. In practical terms, this means: review, repeat and rehearse. Scientific theory suggests that the more we review, repeat and rehearse the information we are trying to remember, the better our chances of recalling that information at a later time. And don't forget about spaced learning! If we wish to optimize memory storage and recall of new learning material, an extended method of time-based learning is more valuable than trying to cram all the new information into one training or study session (see page 168 for more details).

You will have now built a mindset around the principles of the 3R-Axiom. You can use this powerful combination of message, example and activities to make a real difference and impact your audience.

SAM is now waiting for you to re-engage with this book. By doing so, you empower him to continue to make an impact and build or strengthen a mindset. We invite you to a special, exclusive opportunity for readers of this book.

We invite you to become a Mindsetter. As you know, mindsets matter. Our mindset is the key component that drives our success, whether that's personal or professional success. Our mindsets are also a choice. It's a choice we make every day. It's a learned skill, one that can be strengthened and developed. And now that you know the power of the 3R-Axiom, as a Mindsetter you can make a difference in building, encouraging and crafting powerful messages to support the people you care for.

As a Mindsetter, you are not just sharing your message. You are establishing and strengthening mindsets. When you share your mindset, you inspire your friends, community, audience or organization and help others achieve their dreams. We are here to help you replicate that success, over and over again, to the benefit of everyone around you.

Visit www.BeAMindsetter.com today for a very special online tool that we built just for you. Log in, and you'll experience interactive, regular reminders of the concepts you learned in this book. It is the Nth power of the 3R-Axiom, multiplying the power of the axiom and repeating core concepts to ensure SAM survives and you walk away with a true, lasting understanding of how to make messages with impact. SAM is waiting for you right now, so don't waste a single moment!

Then, you can use this same online tool to build and send 3R-enabled messages to friends, family members, colleagues and anyone else who needs to hear your special message. The tool includes easy tutorials and prompts, just in case you're not quite sure how to proceed. Once your own SAM messages are ready, with their examples and activities, this tool lets you send them via email and track responses. And it's not just you. Thousands of other people – other Mindsetters who are passionate about building messages with impact – are making a difference in the lives of others by spreading their messages of change! Join the community and talk to others who have explored this book and use the 3R-Axiom.

It's your turn.

Rescue SAM and become a Mindsetter at **www.BeAMindsetter.com** today!

APPENDIX (1)

THE 3R-AXIOM© AT A GLANCE

1R: Make SAM...

REDUCE what you want to say to a single **SAM** Message to achieve **ATTENTION**

   S = Simple
   A = Applicable
   M = Memorable

2R: Make SAM FIT...

RELATE the message to the audience with a **FIT** Example to create **UNDERSTANDING**

   F = Focused
   I = Inspiring
   T = Tangible

3R: Make SAM FIT for LIFE

Have your audience **REFLECT** on the Example with **LIFE** Activities to ensure **ENGAGEMENT**

   L = Lively
   I = Interactive
   F = Familiar
   E = Envisioning

3R^n: Keep SAM FIT for LIFE

Have your audience **RE-ENGAGE** regularly with more 3R-Messages to support **APPLICATION**

APPENDIX (2)

Meet the Characters

Everything in this book has had a deeper meaning, including the names of each of the characters that SAM meets along the way. You already know what SAM's name represented. Let's explore the purpose and meaning behind the other characters that SAM met during his journey.

SAM's name is an acronym for Simple, Applicable and Memorable.

He is clever and bright. As an illustration example, SAM's glow grows brighter and brighter as each step of the 3R-Axiom is applied to him. SAM seems to be the hero of the story. But this is not quite true, because ultimately you - the sender of the message - deserves that extra credit.

DICK is an acronym for Differentiated, Impersonal, Complex and Kingly.

We portray him as a stormy whirlwind. Like storms, Dick is intense and has also been given a superior expression, as he acts with grandeur and looks down on others. Unfortunately, because Dick is not built with the *simple* rule from the 3R-Axiom, he is quickly taken away by the book's antagonist, The Forgetting.

IGOR's name stands for Implicit, General, Obvious and Redundant.

We portray him as a piece of toast, as he's as interesting and unique as a piece of toasted bread. He is bluff, intrusive and not necessarily the smartest. Unfortunately, because Igor is not built with the *applicable* rule from the 3R-Axiom, he is quickly taken away by The Forgetting.

LUCI stands for Long, Unspecific, Complicated and Interesting.
She is represented as an origami bird. The art of origami takes time and is interesting but complicated. Unfortunately, because Luci is not built with the *memorable* rule from the 3R-Axiom, she is quickly taken away by The Forgetting.

SAMMY is a message just like SAM, but smaller than SAM.
We portray Sammy as a smaller, more junior version of SAM because she has not been supported in her growth with the right example. Her 2R energy drink does not make her strong enough to scale the ladder and get into The Special Place.

SYNAPSO is a friendly, wise character that represents the synapses process in the recipient's brain.
We portray him as an old tree with great roots representing his wisdom and his age. He has been in the brain for a long time, knows many things and helps explain many secrets to SAM, including the secrets of the 3R-Axiom.

THE FORGETTING is a constant threat to the characters you meet in the narrative.
This antagonist represents the process of being forgotten, and nothing is more frightening to the messages in your brain! We portray this dark force as a black square with daunting eyes. It has no real shape and it is lurking everywhere to take hold of any message that has not been crafted and supported according to the principles of the 3R-Axiom.

APPENDIX (3)

(Endnotes)

INTRODUCTION

[1] http://www.radicati.com/wp/wp-content/uploads/2011/05/Email-Statistics-Report-2011-2015-Executive-Summary.pdf

[2] http://www.pewinternet.org/2011/09/19/americans-and-text-messaging/

[3] NeuroLeaderologist. Combines the concepts of Neuroscience and Transformational Leadership with the intent to help leaders leverage brain science to optimize their leadership effectiveness.

CHAPTER 1

[4] Miller, G.A. (1956); The magic number of seven, plus or -2: some limits on our capacity for processing information, *psychological review*, 63, 81-97.

[5] http://abcnews.go.com/Business/kids-mcdonalds-toyota-disney/story?id=10333145

[6] http://www.people.vcu.edu/~tchumley/resources/misc/editing_murch_lecture.pdf

[7] Kare Anderson is a Forbes columnist and Emmy-winning former Wall Street Journal and NBC journalist. Kare has been a public speaker in 18 countries and consultant to companies, sports teams, startups, government leaders and non-profits as diverse as Google, The Skoll Foundation, London School of Economics, Nordstrom, Siemens, Deloitte, and Novartis. For more information, visit Kare's website at: http://www.sayitbetter.com

CHAPTER 2

[8] http://www.johnmaxwell.com/about/meet-john/

[9] Sapolsky, R. M. (1994). *Why zebras don't get ulcers: A guide to stress, stress related diseases, and coping.* New York: W.H. Freeman.

Medina, J. (2008). *Brain rules: 12 principles for surviving and thriving at work, home, and school.* Seattle: Pear Press.

Schwartz, J., & Gladding, R. (2011). You are not your brain: The 4-step solution for changing bad habits, ending unhealthy thinking, and taking control of your life. New York: Avery.

CHAPTER 3

[10] page 110 of Medina's book, *Brain Rules*

[11] The campaign pages are no longer live but if you scroll back to 2012 on the campaign Facebook pages you can see some limited examples. For example, the veterans pages uses war imagery and imagery of veterans: https://www.facebook.com/veteransforobama - https://www.facebook.com/WomenforObama

CHAPTER 4

[12] http://l.kryptoniitti.com/lassial/files/publications/080904-Music_in_everymind_pdf.pdf

[13] http://www.jeffarthur.com/stations/JAPjingle1sheet.pdf

[14] http://adage.com/article/special-report-the-advertising-century/ad-age-advertising-century-top-10-jingles/140154/

[15] http://www.psfk.com/2010/06/singapore-airlines-sensory-branding.html

[16] http://www.nationalcenter.org/GiveMeLiberty.html

[17] Subramaniam, K., Kounios, J., Parrish, T.B., & Jung-Beeman, M. (2009). A brain mechanism for facilitation of insight by positive affect. Journal of Cognitive Neuroscience, 21, 415-432.

Virtue, S., Parrish, T., & Jung-Beeman, M. (2008). Inferences during story comprehension: Cortical recruitment affected by predictability of events and working-memory capacity . Journal of Cognitive Neuroscience, 20, 2274-2284.

Jung-Beeman, M., Collier, A., & Kounios, J. (2008). How insight happens: learning from the brain. NeuroLeadership Journal, 1, 20-25.

Kounios, J. & Jung-Beeman, M. (In press). The Aha! moment: The cognitive neuroscience of insight. Current Directions in Psychological Science.

Jung-Beeman, M., Bowden, E.M., Haberman, J., Frymiare, J.L., Arambel-Liu, S., Greenblatt, R., Reber, P.J., & Kounios, J. (2004). Neural activity observed in people solving verbal problems with insight. Public Library of Science – Biology, 2, 500-510. PLOS Website

[18] http://en.wikipedia.org/wiki/4-H

CHAPTER 5

[19] de Quervain, D. -., & McGaugh, J. L. (2014). Stress and the regulation of memory: From basic mechanisms to clinical implications Neurobiology of Learning and Memory Special Issue. Neurobiology Of Learning And Memory, 1121. doi:10.1016/j.nlm.2014.04.011

Elliot, M. (2013). Finding fun in daily occupation: An investigation of humor. Occupational Therapy in Mental Health, 29(3), 201-214.

Journal of Neuroscience: Weather prediction task: Learning achievement with and without stress. (2012). Biomedical Market Newsletter, 211.

Nelson, C. A., & Carver, L. J. (1998). The effects of stress and trauma on brain and memory: A view from developmental cognitive neuroscience. Development And Psychopathology, 10(4), 793-809. doi:10.1017/S0954579498001874.

Perspectives on Neuroscience and Behaviour. (2014). Neuroscientist, 20(3), 195-196. doi:10.1177/1073858414533653

ROBINSON, O. (., OVERSTREET, C. (., CHARNEY, D. (., VYTAL, K. (., & GRILLON, C. (. (0001). Stress increases aversive prediction error signal in the ventral striatum (English). Proceedings Of The National Academy Of Sciences Of The United States Of America, 110(10), 4129-4133.

[20] Christianson, S.A. (1992). Emotional stress and eyewitness memory: A critical review. Psychological Bulletin, 112(2), 284–309.

Elliot, M. (2013). Finding fun in daily occupation: An investigation of humor. Occupational Therapy in Mental Health, 29(3), 201-214.

Kohn, A. (2004). Feel-bad education. Education Week, 24(3), 44–45.

Pawlak, R., Magarinos, A. M., Melchor, J., McEwen, B., & Strickland, S. (2003). Tissue plasminogen activator in the amygdala is critical for stress-induced anxiety- like behaviour. Nature Neuroscience, 6(2), 168–174.

Thanos, P. K., Katana, J. M., Ashby, C. R., Michaelides, M., Gardner, E. L., Heidbreder, C. A., et al. (1999). The selective dopamine D3 receptor antagonist SB-277011-A attenuates ethanol consumption in ethanol preferring (P) and non- preferring (NP) rats. Pharmacology, Biochemistry, and Behaviour, 81(1), 190–197.

CHAPTER 7

[21] Gale, C., Schroder, T. (2014). Experiences of self-practice/self-reflection in cognitive behavioural therapy: A meta-synthesis of qualitative studies (English). *Psychology And Psychotherapy* [serial online]; 87(4): 373-392.

Smith G, Yates P. The benefits of self-reflection. *Training Journal* [serial online]. November 2012;:49-51. Available from: Health Business Elite, Ipswich, MA. Accessed March 14, 2015.

Kelley, W.M., Macrae, C.N., Wyland, C.L., Caglar, S., Inati, S., and Heatherton, T. (2002). *Finding the Self? An Event-Related fMRI Study.* Journal of Cognitive Neuroscience 2002 14:5, 785-794

Krashen, Stephen D. 1982. *Principles and practice in second language acquisition.* Oxford: Pergamon.

Lieberman, M. (2007). Social Cognitive Neuroscience: A Review of Core Processes. *Annual Review of Psychology*, Vol. 58: 259 -289 (Volume publication date, January 2007).

Ochsner K, Beer J, D'Esposito M, et al. The neural correlates of direct and reflected self-knowledge. *Neuroimage* [serial online]. December 2005;28(4):797-814. Available from: Academic Search Premier, Ipswich, MA. Accessed March 14, 2015.

[22] Same references as the previous end note.

[23] Journaling is a self-reflection exercise aimed at gaining insight into one's experiences, observations, and critical thinking (often in the moment of occurrence or soon after). It is often used as a clinical tool to aid in capturing one's feelings, worldviews, and cognitions related to specific life events. An example of a journal would be a "Gratitude Journal" where one is asked to close their day by self-reflecting on the day's events and capturing (via a journal entries) the day's events they are most thankful for.

Borkin S. (2014). *The Healing Power Of Writing: A Therapist's Guide To Using Journaling With Clients* [e-book]. New York, NY, US: W W Norton & Co.

Evers F. (2008). Journaling: A Path to Our Innermost Self. *Interbeing* [serial online]. 2(2):53-56

Laclaire A. (2009). *The Influence Of Journaling On The Reduction Of Physical Symptoms,*

Health Problems, And Anxiety In Women [e-book]. US: ProQuest Information & Learning.

Lichtenthal W, Neimeyer R. (2012). Directed journaling to facilitate meaning-making. *Techniques of grief therapy: Creative practices for counseling the bereaved* [e-book]. New York, NY, US: Routledge/Taylor & Francis Group:165-168.

Meyer C, Roberts-Cady S, Smith P. (2014). Using Journaling to Inspire Group Reflection on Teaching. *Teaching Professor* [serial online]. 28(8):5.

Murray S. (1997). The benefits of journaling. *Parks & Recreation* [serial online]. 32(5):68.

CHAPTER 8

[24] Bryant P, Coombs A, Pazio M. (2014). Are We Having Fun Yet? Institutional Resistance and the Introduction of Play and Experimentation into Learning Innovation through Social Media. *Journal Of Interactive Media In Education*; (2):32-39.

Murthy, K. (2013). Fun based education for ages from 3 to 100: lighting the candle of learning passion. doi:10.1109/IEDEC.2013.6526751

Somyürek S. (2015). An effective educational tool: construction kits for fun and meaningful learning. *International Journal Of Technology & Design Education*; 25(1):25-41.

[25] Caporello, E. L. (2014). Dealing with distraction: Learning, attention, and the neural encoding of natural auditory scenes. *Dissertation Abstracts International, 74.*

Clark, R. E., & Squire, L. R. (1998). Classical conditioning and brain systems: The role of awareness. *Science, 280*(5360), 77-81.

LaBar, K. S., & Disterhoft, J. F. (1998). Conditioning, awareness, and the hippocampus. *Hippocampus, 8*(6), 620-626. doi:10.1002/(SICI)1098-1063(1998)8:6<620::AID-HIPO4>3.0.CO;2-6.

Marsh, J. E., Sörqvist, P., Hodgetts, H. M., Beaman, C. P., & Jones, D. M. (2015). Distraction control processes in free recall: Benefits and costs to performance. *Journal Of Experimental Psychology: Learning, Memory, And Cognition, 41*(1), 118-133. doi:10.1037/a0037779.

Naveh-Benjamin, M., Guez, J., Hara, Y., Brubaker, M. S., & Lowenschuss-Erlich, I. (2014). The effects of divided attention on encoding processes under incidental and intentional learning instructions: Underlying mechanisms?. *Quarterly Journal Of Experimental Psychology, 67*(9), 1682-1696. doi:10.1080/17470218.2013.867517.

Szpunar. K., Khan, N., Schacter, D. (2014). Interpolated memory tests reduce mind wandering and improve learning of online lectures (English). *Proceedings Of The National Academy Of Sciences Of The United States Of America, 110*(16), 6313-6317.

VanWormer, L. A., Bireta, T. J., Surprenant, A. M., & Neath, I. (2012). The Effect of Perceptual Cues on Inhibiting Irrelevant Information in Older Adults Using a List-Learning Method. *Experimental Aging Research, 38*(3), 279-294. doi:10.1080/036107 3X.2012.672131.

Zeamer, C., & Fox Tree, J. E. (2013). The process of auditory distraction: Disrupted attention and impaired recall in a simulated lecture environment. *Journal Of Experimental Psychology: Learning, Memory, And Cognition, 39*(5), 1463-1472. doi:10.1037/a0032190.

[26] Bristow, D., Dehaene-Lambertz, G., Mattout, J., Soares, C., Gliga1, 4. T., Baillet, S., & Mangin, J. (2009). Hearing Faces: How the Infant Brain Matches the Face It Sees with the Speech It Hears. *Journal Of Cognitive Neuroscience, 21*(5), 905-921.

Ellamil, M., Dobson, C., Beeman, M., and Christoff, K. (2011). Evaluative and generative modes of thought during the creative process. *Neuroimage 59*, 1783–1794. doi: 10.1016/j.neuroimage.2011.08.008

Kolb, B., & Whishaw, I. Q. (2003). *Fundamentals of human neuropsychology (5th ed.).* New York, NY, US: Worth Publishers.

O'Reilly, R. (2001). Generalization in interactive networks: the benefits of inhibitory competition and Hebbian learning. *Neural Computation, 13*(6), 1199-1241.

Ramachandran, V. S.; Hubbard, E. M. (2001), "Synaesthesia: A window into perception, thought and language", *Journal of Consciousness Studies* **8** (12): 3–34

Endslay, Mica R. (2004). Simon Banbury, Sébastien Tremblay, ed. *A Cognitive Approach To Situation Awareness: Theory and Application* (1st ed.). USA: Ashgate Publishing, Ltd. ISBN 0-7546-4198-8.

Conrad, Klaus (1958). *Die beginnende Schizophrenie; Versuch einer Gestaltanalyse des Wahns* (in German). Stuttgart: Thieme. OCLC 14620263.

Sherlock, P. (2008). "On roulette wheels and monkies randomly inspired by Shakespeare". truth.gooberbear. Retrieved 2008-04-01.

Gibson, William (2003). *Pattern Recognition*. New York: G. P. Putnam's Sons. ISBN 978-0-3991-4986-3. OCLC 49894062.

[27] http://ctl.utexas.edu/preparing/node/36

[28] http://www.athleticinsight.com/Vol6Iss1/MentalSkillsReview.htm

CHAPTER 9

[29] Many scholars and researchers posit differing views on the mechanics of memory. From Théodule-Armand Ribot (1839-1916) to William James (1842-1910) to Hermann Ebbinghaus (1850-1909) to Richard Semon (1859-1918) to Donald Hebb (1904-1985), all have made significant contributions to the scientific field of memory. More recently, and with the help of new and advanced technology such as the fMRI (functional magnetic resonance imaging), many neuroscientists, psychologists and memory scholars (e.g., Eric Kandel, George Miller, Daniel Schacter, John Medina, and Elizabeth Loftus) have continued to make huge gains in our understanding of how memory is believed to be encoded, stored and retrieved.

[30] http://www.unm.edu/~lkravitz/Article%20folder/resistben.html

ACKNOWLEDGEMENTS

We are humbled and grateful to the significant contributions made by the many people who supported us and helped us make this book a reality.

We would like to extend a very special thank you to Joshua Duvauchelle for his absolutely unbelievable support in writing this book. Without him, we would not have been able to navigate through this journey. He worked closely with us to bring all of our ideas and thoughts to life and turn them into readable, understandable and consistent narratives.

We also want to thank Christian Haarmann, whose incredible design expertise set the initial design foundations for this book. His creative vision was instrumental in our initial layouts and brainstorming.

Additionally, we were so fortunate to work with Jürgen Diessl (ECON), who connected us to Martin Liu of LID Publishing and facilitated our relationship with them.

We also extend a special thank you to David Woods, Laura Hawkins, Sara Taheri and their colleagues at LID Publishing for their unbounded creativity and excellent publishing advice. They provided amazingly efficient and professional support in editing and designing this book.

In addition to the names above, we would like to personally thank all of our family, friends, and colleagues who have supported our SAM journey and whose guidance, wisdom and insights have proved invaluable towards the success of this book.

Finally, we are deeply grateful to the team at Mindsetter.com for their technical support in providing the online companion experience to this book – a series of mindtriggers that empower readers like you to continue to engage with the ideas and lessons you're holding in your hands.

MICHAEL GOBRAN

Michael Gobran founded and served as CEO of two European enterprises. Since the 1990s, he has focused on training and consulting and launched an online learning platform using the 3R-Axiom, to help individuals inspire, influence and impact others. For more than 20 years, Gobran has focused on change management, leadership and strategy. Clients, such as Bayer, Allianz and BMW turn to him for expertise in ensuring employees and customers hear and understand their messages.

WILLIAM GREENWALD

William Greenwald is founder and Chief Neuroleaderologist at the Windsor Leadership Group, specializing in the neuropsychology of team and leadership behavior. He is completing his graduate training in clinical psychology at Harvard University and holds two master's degrees from the University of Pennsylvania. He is the "go to" educator and coach on Servant Leadership and Neuroleadership and lectures at universities, including Wharton Business School. He delivers keynote presentations worldwide.

DEREK ROBERTS

Derek Roberts is an Executive Partner with Integrity Solutions, President of Roberts Business Group and co-founder of the Institute for Impact. His expertise is in organizational leadership development and the establishment of high-performance sales and service cultures. As a professional communication consultant, international speaker and executive coach, Derek works closely with billion dollar organizations like American Red Cross and Border States Electric to help shape and execute their leadership and growth strategies.